Michael Price

Windows 7
for Seniors

For the Over 50s

In easy steps is an imprint of In Easy Steps Limited
Southfield Road · Southam
Warwickshire CV47 0FB · United Kingdom
www.ineasysteps.com

Notice of Liability
Every effort has been made to ensure that this book
contains accurate and current information. However, In
Easy Steps Limited and the author shall not be liable for
any loss or damage suffered by readers as a result of
any information contained herein.

Trademarks
All trademarks are acknowledged as belonging to their
respective companies.

In Easy Steps Limited supports The Forest Stewardship
Council (FSC), the leading international forest certification
organisation. All our titles that are printed on Greenpeace
approved FSC certified paper carry the FSC logo.

Mixed Sources
Product group from well-managed
forests and other controlled sources
www.fsc.org Cert no. SGS-COC-005998
© 1996 Forest Stewardship Council

Printed and bound in the United Kingdom

ISBN 978-1-84078-386-5

Contents

4   Taskbar and Start Menu   57

5   Gadgets and Devices   75

8 Internet 135

9 Windows Applications 153

1 Get Windows 7

This chapter will help you choose the best edition of Windows 7 for you. It compares the features and covers upgrading from a previous version of Windows, or moving up to a more advanced edition of Windows 7.

Windows 7

Don't forget

There have been other releases of Microsoft Windows, intended for business and server computers, including Windows NT, Windows 2000, Windows Server 2003 and Windows Server 2008.

Windows 7 is the latest release of Microsoft Windows, the operating system for personal computers. There has been a long list of Windows releases including:

- 1995 Windows 95
- 1998 Windows 98
- 2000 Windows Me (Millennium Edition)
- 2001 Windows XP (eXPerience)
- 2003 Windows XP MCE (Media Center Edition)
- 2007 Windows Vista
- 2009 Windows 7

When you buy a new computer, it is usually shipped with the latest available release of Windows. This takes advantage of the hardware features generally available at the time. Every year sees new and more powerful features being incorporated into the latest computers. In line with this, the requirements for Microsoft Windows have increased steadily. For example, the minimum and recommended amounts of system memory have increased from Windows 95 (4 MB to 8 MB), Windows 98 (16 MB to 24 MB), Windows XP (64 MB to 128 MB), Windows Vista (512 MB to 1024 MB) and now Windows 7 (1 GB to 2 GB). There's a similar progression in terms of the processor power, the video graphics facilities and hard disk storage.

This means that your computer is likely to need upgrading in order to use a later release of Windows, unless you purchased your computer late in the life of the previous release and it already meets the newer requirements.

Hot tip

If you purchased a Windows Vista PC after June 26th 2009, you may be entitled to a free upgrade to Windows 7.

The extended hardware options allow the features and services offered by the various releases of Windows to be developed and improved. Each release enhances the existing features and adds new capabilities. Windows 7 is therefore able to provide all of the capabilities of Windows Vista and Windows XP, and also offer unique new features.

The value of all this is that you can use your computer to carry out tasks that would not have been possible with previous computers and operating system releases.

Which Release is Installed?

To check which release of Windows is currently installed on your system, you can look in System Properties.

1 Press the Windows Logo key and the Break key (simultaneously) to display the System Properties

2 The operating system details will be displayed (along with user, memory and processor information)

The layout varies between releases of Windows, but similar details are shown.

Windows XP

Windows Vista

Windows 7

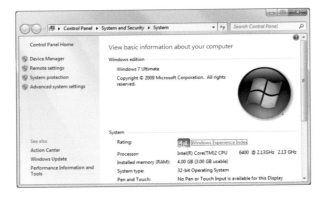

Hot tip

You can also open System Properties from the Control Panel, or you can right-click the Computer icon and select Properties.

Don't forget

This shows the system properties (on the same computer) for Windows XP, Windows Vista and Windows 7.

11

Hot tip

Note that there is 4 GB installed, but Windows only uses 3 GB (except when you have a 64-bit edition installed).

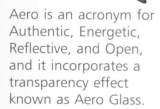

Hot tip

Aero is an acronym for Authentic, Energetic, Reflective, and Open, and it incorporates a transparency effect known as Aero Glass.

Don't forget

Some programs can add relevant tasks to their Jump Lists. For example, Windows Media Player has options to Play All Music or to resume your last playlist. Internet Explorer offers frequently visited and recently viewed websites.

Features of Windows 7

Taskbar and Previews

You can pin any program to the taskbar so it's always ready to use. When you have started a program, hover over the taskbar button and you'll see thumbnails of every window open in that program. Hover over one of the thumbnails, and the Aero Peek feature lets you see a full-screen preview of that window. Move the cursor off the thumbnail and the full-screen preview disappears.

Jump Lists

The new Jump List feature allows you to access the documents you've used recently, when you right-click the associated program's task button on the taskbar. If there are other files you want to access quickly, you can pin them to the Jump List so they always appear.

Desktop enhancements

Windows 7 offers new ways to handle the windows on your desktop. For example, the Snap feature lets you pull a window to either side edge of the screen to fill half the screen. You can Snap windows to both sides of the screen, to make it easy to compare those windows.

To clear your desktop, just move your mouse to the lower right corner of your desktop. Using the Aero Peek feature, the open Windows become transparent, so you can see the shortcuts and gadgets on your desktop. There's also an Aero Shake function. Grab the top of one window and shake it, all the other open windows will minimize to the taskbar. Shake the window again, and they'll all come back.

Aero Themes let you personalize the background, color, sound and screen saver used on your system, with a single selection from a range of interesting styles, or you can customize your own theme.

Windows Search

Windows Search helps you find anything on your PC quickly and easily, using the search box at the bottom of the Start menu. Windows 7 libraries show all content of a particular type in one spot, and Windows Search makes it even simpler to find items, with filters to customize your search.

Internet Explorer 8

The latest version of the Windows web browser, Internet Explorer 8 features innovations to the address bar, search, tabs, and the Favorites bar. For example, as you type a search request you'll immediately start seeing relevant suggestions from your chosen search provider, complete with images when available.

HomeGroup

HomeGroup is set up automatically when you add the first PC running Windows 7 to your home network. When you add more PCs running Windows 7 to the home network, they join the HomeGroup, and they can share files and printers with each other.

View Available Network (VAN)

Windows 7 makes viewing and connecting to all of your networks simple and consistent, whether the networks are based on Wi-Fi, mobile broadband, dial-up or your company's VPN.

Windows Touch

With a touch-screen monitor, you touch your computer screen to scroll, resize windows, play media, pan and zoom. The Start menu, Windows Taskbar, Windows Explorer and Internet Explorer are all touch-enabled. Windows 7 also supports multi-touch technology, where you control what happens on the screen with more than one finger, using a variety of gestures.

Windows Live Essentials

Windows Live Essentials provides features that were included in previous versions of Windows Vista. You can download the latest releases of those programs from the Internet, and also integrate what you do on your PC with associated online services.

Hot tip

Search uses your browsing history to narrow the list of suggestions. When you see what you're looking for, you can select that item from the list.

13

Beware

Some features are only available in particular editions of Windows 7, or have specific hardware prerequisites.

What's Needed

The minimum configuration recommended by Microsoft to install and run Windows 7 is as follows:

- Processor   1 GHz 32-bit or 64-bit
- System memory   1 GB (32-bit) or 2 GB (64-bit)
- Graphics   DirectX 9 graphics device with WDDM 1.0 driver
- Hard disk drive   16 GB (32-bit) or 20 GB (64-bit) free
- Optical drive   DVD/CD (for installation purposes)

There may be additional requirements for some features, for example:

- SVGA display monitor with 1024x768 or higher resolution is recommended for some applications

- Internet access, for online services and features such as Windows Update

- TV tuner, for Windows Media Center functions

- Touch specific hardware, for touch functions

- A network and multiple PCs running Windows 7, for HomeGroup file and printer sharing

- An optical drive with rewriter function, for DVD/CD authoring and backup function

- Trusted Platform Module (TPM) 1.2 hardware for BitLocker encryption

- USB flash drive, for BitLocker To Go

- An additional 1 GB memory, 15 GB extra hard disk space, and a processor with Intel VT or AMD-V hardware virtualization, for Windows XP Mode

- Audio output (headphones or speakers), for music and sound in Windows Media Center or Media Player

Upgrade Advisor

To have your computer assessed to see if it is able to support Windows 7, visit the website www.microsoft.com/windows/windows-7/get/upgrade-advisor.aspx and click the link to download the Windows 7 Upgrade Advisor.

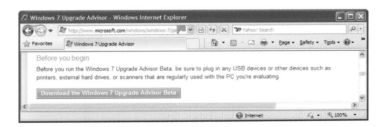

Run this program to install the Upgrade Advisor and follow the prompts to install and launch the program. This will generate a report to tell you if any changes are needed to support Windows 7 on your computer. It also identifies any incompatible software or accessories that you may have.

For example, when run on an Asus Eee PC netbook computer currently running Windows XP, the Upgrade Advisor says that this passes all four system requirements.

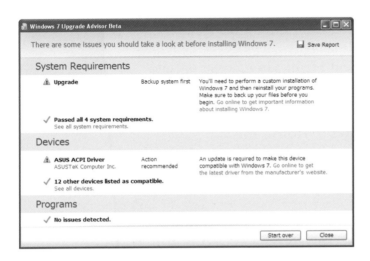

However, you are warned that you need to perform a custom installation of Windows 7, then reinstall your programs. Upgrade from Windows XP to Windows 7 is not supported.

Hot tip

If your computer runs Windows XP or Vista, it may already be able to run Windows 7, perhaps with a hardware upgrade. Computers running earlier versions of Windows are unlikely to have the necessary capabilities.

Beware

An update to the ACPI driver is recommended, though this would happen automatically when you carry out the full installation.

Windows 7 Editions

There are six editions of Windows 7, with each edition being a superset of the one after it in the list.

Windows 7 Ultimate
Ultimate is available as a retail package and for pre-install, but is not volume-licensed. It has the full set of Windows 7 features, the same as the Enterprise edition.

Windows 7 Enterprise
Enterprise is for volume-license business use only, and is not supplied as a retail package or for pre-install.

Features exclusive to the Ultimate and Enterprise editions include security features such as AppLocker and BitLocker, plus support for multilingual user interfaces.

Windows 7 Professional
Professional is provided as a retail package and for pre-install. It includes Backup to Network and XP Mode licensing features.

Windows 7 Home Premium
Home Premium is for retail and pre-install. It supports Aero Glass, Windows Touch and Home Group creation, and includes Windows Media Center and Premium games.

Windows 7 Home Basic
This is for emerging markets only. It includes Fast User Switching, Internet Connection Sharing, Network Bridge and Mobility Center (but without Presentation Mode).

Windows 7 Starter
This is available worldwide, for pre-install only. As with Home Basic, Home Group support is join-only, not create. In a final constraint, Starter has no support for Personalization, so you cannot change the desktop background or theme.

Selecting your Edition

If you are unsure which of these editions of Windows 7 is best for you, it's worth focusing on the features that are included or excluded from one or other edition.

Feature	ST	HB	HP	PR	E/U
Aero Peek, Shake, Glass	-	-	Y	Y	Y
AppLocker , BitLocker	-	-	-	-	Y
Backup to network	-	-	-	Y	Y
Boot from VHD	-	-	-	-	Y
Dolby Digital compatibility	-	-	Y	Y	Y
DVD playback	-	-	Y	Y	Y
Encrypting File System	-	-	-	Y	Y
Fast User Switching	-	Y	Y	Y	Y
Federated Search	-	-	-	-	Y
HomeGroup creation	-	-	Y	Y	Y
IIS Web Server	-	-	Y	Y	Y
Internet Connection Sharing	-	Y	Y	Y	Y
Live Taskbar Previews	-	Y	Y	Y	Y
Multilingual UI packs	-	-	-	-	Y
Multi-Touch, Tablet PC	-	-	Y	Y	Y
Network Bridge	-	Y	Y	Y	Y
Premium games	-	-	Y	Y	Y
Remote Desktop Host	-	-	-	Y	Y
Snipping Tool, Sticky Notes	-	-	Y	Y	Y
Windows DVD Maker	-	-	Y	Y	Y
Windows Flip 3D	-	-	Y	Y	Y
Windows Journal	-	-	Y	Y	Y
Windows Media Center	-	-	Y	Y	Y
Windows Sideshow	-	-	Y	Y	Y
XP Mode licensed	-	-	-	Y	Y

If any of these features are ones that you must have, this will dictate the editions that you need to investigate in more detail. In practice, the choice for home use is normally between the Home Premium and Professional editions, with the Ultimate edition being the alternative for the full home and business features. For travelling, you may find a netbook with Starter edition pre-installed will meet your needs.

Don't forget

The six editions of Windows 7 are:
ST	Starter
HB	Home Basic
HP	Home Premium
PR	Professional
E	Enterprise
U	Ultimate

17

Hot tip

If you choose a lower function edition and discover you do need additional features, you have the opportunity to upgrade your edition to a higher level (see page 18).

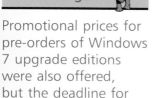
Upgrades

If you are planning to install Windows 7 on an existing computer running Windows XP or Windows 2000, you can purchase an upgrade copy rather than the full copy. The contents are the same, but you pay a reduced price because you are replacing a qualifying operating system.

As an indication of the relative cost of the editions and the saving with an upgrade, the US$ prices at launch time were:

- Home Premium $199.99 $119.99

- Professional $299.99 $199.99

- Ultimate $319.99 $219.99

Microsoft also announced a Windows 7 Family pack which provides three upgrade licenses of the Home Premium edition. This is being made available at a promotional price of $149.99.

Whichever edition of Windows 7 you choose, the DVD supplied actually contains all the editions. It is the product key that unlocks your particular edition. This gives you another option – the Windows Anytime Upgrade.

- Starter   → Home Premium $79.99

- Starter   → Professional $114.99

- Starter   → Ultimate $164.99

- Home Premium   → Professional $89.99

- Home Premium   → Ultimate $139.99

- Professional   → Ultimate $129.99

Whether you buy the WAU retail package from a store or make your purchase online from Windows 7, the upgrade takes only 10 or 15 minutes. No DVD is required – all you need is the upgrade key. Your current programs, files, and settings will remain intact.

1 Select Start, Control Panel and System and Security

System and Security
Review your computer's status
Back up your computer
Find and fix problems
View basic information about
your computer

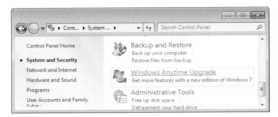

Hot tip

In this example, the current configuration is Starter which can be upgraded to Home Premium, Professional or Ultimate.

2 Scroll down and select Windows Anytime Upgrade

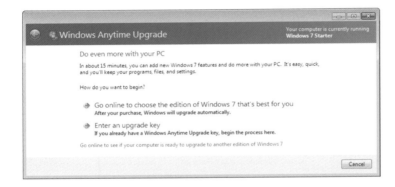

Hot tip

You can choose to go online to see if your computer is ready to upgrade. This allows you to download and run the Windows 7 Upgrade Advisor (see page 15).

3 Choose to select and purchase an edition online, or to enter and verify your WAU upgrade key

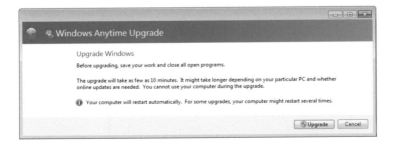

Don't forget

The upgrade will not change your settings and data or remove programs. However, it is still best to ensure that you have a current backup (see page 232).

4 Follow the prompts to upgrade to the new edition

19

32-Bit versus 64-Bit

The 64-bit processor can handle large amounts of memory. However, this does depend on having the 64-bit version of the Windows operating system installed. Otherwise, the processor would be subject to the 32-bit restrictions.

This table shows the editions of Windows 7 that offer 64-bit versions, and the maximum memory they support.

Processor type	ST	HB	HP	PR	E/U
32-bit	Y	Y	Y	Y	Y
Max memory (GB)	4	4	4	4	4
64-bit	-	-	Y	Y	Y
Max memory (GB)	-	-	16	192	192

To check which Windows you are currently running:

1 Open the System Properties (see page 11) to see the system type currently installed

Asus Eee PC   Dell E520

System		
Rating:	2.1 Windows Experience Index	4.1 Windows Experience Index
Processor:	Intel(R) Atom(TM) CPU N280 1.66GHz 1.67 GHz	Intel(R) Core(TM)2 CPU 6400 @ 2.13GHz 2.13 GHz
Installed memory (RAM):	1.00 GB	4.00 GB (3.00 GB usable)
System type:	32-bit Operating System	32-bit Operating System
Pen and Touch:	No Pen or Touch Input is available for this Display	No Pen or Touch Input is available for this Display

2 Click Windows Experience Index, then click View and print detailed performance and system information

View and print detailed performance and system information

Asus Eee PC   Dell E520

System		
Manufacturer	ASUSTeK Computer INC.	Dell Inc.
Model	1000HE	Dell DM061
Total amount of system memory	1.00 GB RAM	4.00 GB RAM
System type	32-bit operating system	32-bit operating system
Number of processor cores	1	2
64-bit capable	No	Yes

3 This says whether or not the system is 64-bit capable

Don't forget

The hardware requirements for Windows 7 (see page 14) specify a 32-bit or 64-bit processor. These terms relate to the way the processor handles memory.

Hot tip

The retail packages have DVDs for both types of processor. The supplied product key can be used with either, but once activated, it will be restricted to that particular computer.

Don't forget

Here the ASUS Eee PC Netbook is 32-bit only, while the Dell E520, though it has a 32-bit system installed, is actually 64-bit capable.

Where the computer already has a 64-bit operating system installed, System Properties shows this, and so the details do not need to explicitly state the computer is 64-bit capable.

System		
Rating:	⬛4.1 Windows Experience Index	
Processor:	Intel(R) Core(TM)2 CPU 6400 @ 2.13GHz 2.13 GHz	
Installed memory (RAM):	4.00 GB	
System type:	64-bit Operating System	
Pen and Touch:	No Pen or Touch Input is available for this Display	

Manufacturer	Dell Inc.
Model	Dell DM061
Total amount of system memory	4.00 GB RAM
System type	64-bit operating system
Number of processor cores	2

Maximum Physical Memory
One final thing to check is the maximum physical memory that can be installed in your computer. This is usually less than the operating system supports, for example:

Make and Model	Type `	Max Memory
ASUS Eee 1000HE	Netbook	2 GB
ASUS V4P5P43	Desktop	8 GB
ASUS RS161-E5/PA2	Server	64 GB

The benefits of 64-bit processing will become apparent when you have 4 GB or more memory installed in your computer and when you are running several programs at the same time and switching between them.

You'll get further benefits with applications optimized for 64-bit processing. Games for example often include such enhancements. The new version of Microsoft is also available in 64-bit, as are video products such as Adobe Photoshop.

You'll still be able to run 32-bit applications under the 64-bit operating system, though this might slow down due to the need to convert addresses.

However, remember that the existing 32-bit drivers for your devices will not run under the 64-bit operating system, so you must ensure that you can get 64-bit versions of the drivers. You may find this a problem when you want to attach older devices to your computer.

Beware

Choosing a 64-bit system means that you can no longer run 16-bit applications. This would only be a problem if you use very old software.

Activation

Activation is the process by which Microsoft associates your specific copy of Windows 7 with your computer.

Your copy of Windows 7 must be activated before you can apply an upgrade, and in any event within 30 days of first using the system. To check the current status:

1 Open the System Properties (see page 11)

2 Scroll to the bottom of the System details to view the Windows Activation status

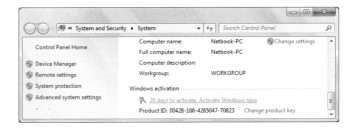

If Activation was specified when your system was installed, it will be completed automatically three days after first use.

3 If your copy of Windows 7 is not yet activated, click Activate Windows Now and follow the prompts

4 When this completes, System Properties will now show the status as Activated

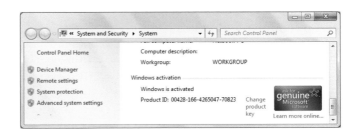

2 The Windows 7 Desktop

The Getting Started panel in Windows 7 introduces you to the Windows 7 user interface with its enhanced Taskbar and improved window structure and control, especially the Snap capability for moving and resizing windows.

Start Windows 7

Switch on your computer to start up the operating system. The stages are as follows:

1 The moving logo with the Starting Windows message shows that the system is being loaded

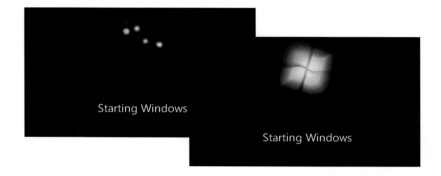

Starting Windows

Starting Windows

2 After a while, the screen clears, the Startup sound plays and the Logon screen is displayed

Michael

Password

Windows 7 Ultimate

3 Enter your password (if one has been defined) then press Enter or click the Forward arrow to sign on

Hot tip

The start-up time depends on the configuration of your computer but usually it will be a minute or so.

Don't forget

If your system has multiple user accounts they will be displayed for you, select the one you want to use.

4 The Welcome message is displayed while the user account settings are being applied

Hot tip

If there is only one user account and no password is assigned, Windows skips the Logon screen and goes straight to this Welcome message.

5 The Windows desktop is displayed, with various Windows components, e.g. Taskbar and Gadgets

Desktop Icons   Windows Background   Windows Gadgets

Getting Started (Live Thumbnail)

Show Desktop

Start Button   Shortcuts Pinned to Taskbar   Active Task   Notification Area

Don't forget

The specific Windows components displayed will depend on the way in which your system is personalized (see page 40).

25

Getting Started

Getting Started gives a list of tasks you may want to carry out when you set up your computer, for example:

Don't forget

Getting Started has similar functions to those included in the Welcome Center that displayed when you started Windows Vista.

- Transfer files and settings from another computer
- Add new users to your computer
- Backup your files and folders
- Personalize your desktop

1 Click Start then Getting Started, at the top of the Start menu

26

Hot tip

This screens shows Aero effects such as shadows and transparency. Future screenshots will use a plain white desktop, and avoid overlaying windows and icons, to help clarify the illustrations.

Click any of these options to see an outline of the functions and a link to open the option, or just double-click an option to open it immediately. For example:

1 Click Personalize Windows to choose a theme for desktop, color and sound (see page 40)

2 Go online to get Windows Live Essentials (see page 37) and download Windows Live Mail, etc

3 Click the Close button to finish working with Getting Started

Start Menu

The usual way to locate Windows applications and functions is from the Start menu. To display the Start menu:

1 Click the Start button on the left of the Taskbar, or press the Windows Logo key on the keyboard

Hot tip

The box at the side of entries such as Paint and Notepad tells you there's a Jump List which will list recently accessed documents.

Default has no fixed entries

Recently used entries

Recently added

Search box

Current user

Folders

Settings

Shutdown

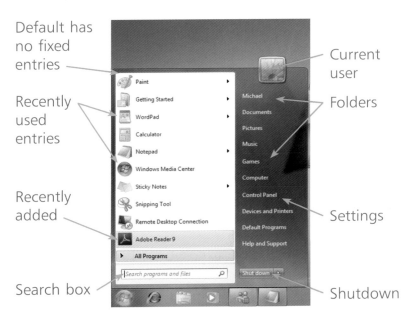

2 Click an entry to open it

3 Type in the Search box to find a file or a program (see page 113)

4 Click All Programs (which changes to Back) then locate the item needed from the lists that are displayed and click to open it

Don't forget

When you Search, the results are listed on the Start menu in the area used for Fixed and Recently used entries. When you select All Programs or one of its subfolders, the contents are listed in that same area.

Taskbar

The contents of the Taskbar change dynamically to reflect the activities that are taking place on your computer.

There are a number of components shown on the Taskbar.

Task Buttons

There is a task button for each open window (program or file folder). The selected or foreground task, in this case the Calculator, is shown emphasized. The other tasks are shaded.

Taskbar Shortcuts

Between the Start button and the task buttons, you'll find shortcuts  that turn into task buttons when you select them to start a program. By default, there are shortcuts for Internet Explorer, Windows Explorer and Windows Media Player, but you can pin any program here.

Notification Area

The portion of the bar on the right is know as the Notification Area and  contains icons such as Action Center, Network, Speaker and Date/Time. These are system functions that are started automatically when Windows starts up. To the right of the notification area is the Show Desktop button (see page 61).

Language Bar

To the left of the notification area you may find the Language bar. This appears when you add a second input language or speech recognition, or even the simple situation of two English inputs – United States and United Kingdom – required perhaps to support an alternative keyboard.

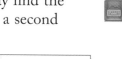

see page 61

Hot tip

The right edge of the frame around the task button tells you the number of windows:

One window
Two windows
Three or more

Don't forget

Click the button to show hidden icons, in this case for USB drive, Printer and Antivirus software.

...cont'd

If you start more tasks, the Taskbar may become full, and scrolling arrows will be added to let you select any task.

You can resize the Taskbar, but first it must be unlocked.

1 Right-click an empty part of the Taskbar and, if there's a check next to Lock the Taskbar, click the entry to remove the check and unlock the Taskbar

2 Move the mouse over the edge of the Taskbar until the pointer becomes a double-headed arrow, then drag the border up or down to resize the Taskbar

3 You can lock the Taskbar at the new size if you wish

You can add other toolbars to the Taskbar:

1 Right-click an empty part of the Taskbar and select Toolbars

2 Select a toolbar and a tick will be added, and the toolbar will be displayed on the Taskbar

Hot tip

See page 58 for more details on customizing the Taskbar and the Start Menu.

Don't forget

This right-click menu is also used to arrange windows (see page 65) or display the Taskbar and Start menu Properties.

Desktop Icons

Shortcuts to frequently used tasks can also be stored on the desktop. To start with there are standard system icons.

You can change the desktop icons from the default size Medium to Large as shown here, or to Small.

1 To display or resize icons on the desktop, right-click an empty part of the desktop and select View

2 If the entry Show desktop icons is not already selected (ticked) then click to enable it

3 To specify which system icons to display, right-click the desktop and select Personalize

Click the Change Icon button to select alternative images for any of the system icons. Click Restore Default to revert to the original images.

4 Click Change Desktop Icons

5 Select the icons that you wish to display then click OK to apply the changes

Window Structure

When you open a folder or start a Windows function, or application program, the contents appear on the screen as a window. Windows 7 introduces some new features to these windows. To view a typical window:

 Select Start, and click the Documents folder link

Don't forget

Not all the Windows applications use the new style. See page 155-156 for examples of more conventional windows.

Features of Windows

Forward and Back buttons

Address bar

Title bar area

Minimize and Maximize buttons

Close button

Search box

Command bar

Library pane

Headings

Contents pane

Details pane

Navigation pane

Horizontal scroll bar

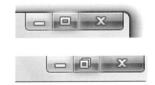 Click the Maximize button to view the window using the whole screen, and the Restore button will appear in its place

Application Windows

Application programs, even ones included in Windows 7, may use the traditional window structure, with Title bar and Menu bar. For example, the Notepad application window.

1 Select Start, All Programs, Accessories and Notepad then type some text (or open an existing file)

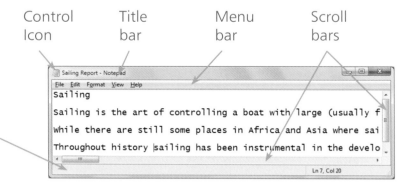

Control Icon   Title bar   Menu bar   Scroll bars

Status bar (with cursor location)

Other Windows 7 applications such as Paint and WordPad feature the Scenic Ribbon in place of menu bar and toobar.

1 Select Start, All Programs, Accessories and WordPad then open a file (or type some text)

WordPad button   Quick Access toolbar   Tabs   Scenic ribbon

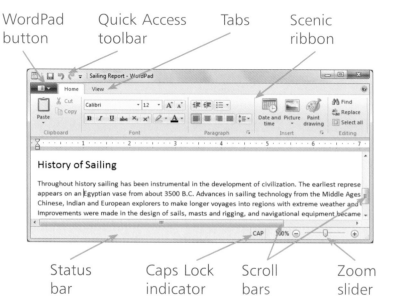

Status bar   Caps Lock indicator   Scroll bars   Zoom slider

Don't forget

Some applications may not use all the features. For example, the Calculator window has no scroll bars and also cannot be resized.

32

Menus and Dialogs

The entries on the Command bar and on the Menu bar expand to provide a list of related commands to pick from. Some entries expand into a submenu, for example

1 In a folder window, select Organize and then Layout

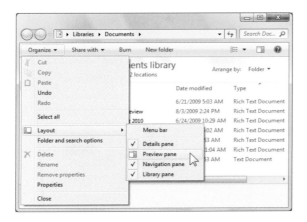

Other entries open dialog boxes that allow you to apply more complex configurations and settings, for example

2 Select Organize and then Folder and search options

3 Make changes and click OK to apply, or click Restore Defaults to undo

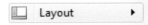

Move and Resize Windows

1 To maximize the window, double-click the title bar area (double-click again to restore the window)

2 To move the window, click the title bar area, hold down the mouse button and drag the window

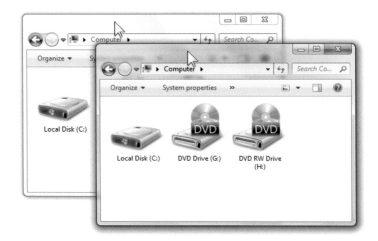

3 To resize the window, move the mouse pointer over any border or any corner

4 When the double-headed resize arrow appears, click and drag until the window is the desired size

Snap

New to Windows 7, the Snap feature offers ways to move and resize windows in one step.

Maximize the Window

1 Drag the title bar to the top of the screen

2 The window's outline expands to fill the whole desktop

3 Release the title bar to maximize the window

Expand Vertically

1 Drag the top border of the window to the top of the screen

2 The window's outline expands to the height of the desktop

3 Release the title bar to maximize the height but maintain the width of the window

Compare Two Windows

1 Drag the title bar to the left of the screen

2 Release and the window expands to fill half the desktop

3 Repeat with a second window, dragging the title bar to the right, and you'll be able to view side by side

Don't forget

Although this feature is also known as Aero Snaps, it is available in all editions of Windows 7 and does not rely on Aero capability.

Hot tip

To return a window to its original size, drag the title bar away from the top of the desktop and then release.

Close Windows Session

When you are ready to end your Windows session, click the Start button and you'll be offered several options.

1 Select Shutdown to close all open programs, shut down Windows and turn off your computer

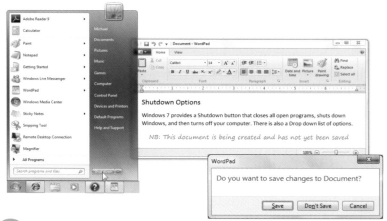

Shutdown Options

Windows 7 provides a Shutdown button that closes all open programs, shuts down Windows, and then turns off your computer. There is also a Drop down list of options.

NB: This document is being created and has not yet been saved

WordPad

Do you want to save changes to Document?

Save | Don't Save | Cancel

2 Save changes to any open documents if prompted, before shutting down

3 Alternatively, click the down arrow next to Shutdown to select an option from the list provided

Switch User	keep current session and open new
Log Off	end the current session
Lock	password protect the current session
Restart	shut down and restart Windows
Sleep	save session and set low-power mode
Hibernate	save the session and power off
Shut Down	end the session and power off

36

Not all computers offer all the options, for example Sleep or Hibernate may be missing or disabled. Also, the Switch User option is not supported under Starter edition.

Get Windows Live Essentials

1 Select Getting Started and then Go online to get Windows Live Essentials

2 Select the language then click Download

3 Choose Run for the setup program

4 Select the programs then click Install

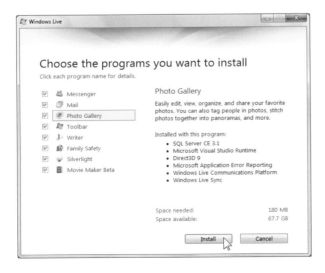

Hot tip

Unlike previous versions of Windows, Windows 7 doesn't include applications such as Windows Mail and Photo Gallery. However, you can download Windows Live equivalents at no charge.

Don't forget

Windows Live will also include the associated programs and utilities that are needed for the applications that you select.

...cont'd

5 If required, Windows Live prompts you to close open applications before proceeding

6 The selected applications are downloaded and then installed in turn

7 When the install ends, create your Windows Live ID

3 Personalize Your System

Change the appearance of the Windows 7 desktop. Take advantage of Aero themes if your system supports these. The options for non-Aero editions are also covered. Select mouse and display features and explore the usability options in the Ease of Access center.

Personalize with Themes

The Personalization function allows you to customize various items on your system, including desktop features and mouse pointers.

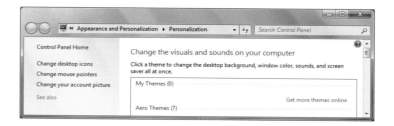

Hot tip

You'll also find links to Personalization in the Getting Started and in Appearance and Personalization in the Control Panel (see page 90).

1 Right-click a clear part of the desktop (avoiding icons and gadgets) and select Personalize

2 This opens Personalization from the Control Panel

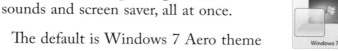

Don't forget

With Windows 7 Starter and Home Basic editions, the Personalization option is not supported, and the Personalize entry does not appear on the right-click menu.

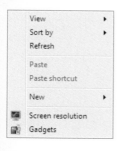

Here you change desktop background, windows color, sounds and screen saver, all at once.

3 The default is Windows 7 Aero theme

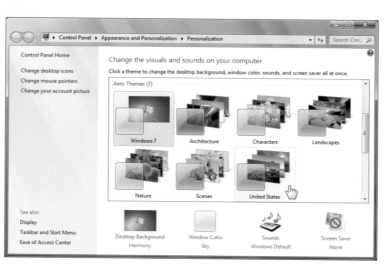

4 Select your location specific theme e.g. United States

5 The selected theme is applied immediately, and a sample of the associated sound scheme is played

6 The components of the selected scheme are displayed at the foot of the Personalization panel

7 The theme is applied, so just Close Personalization to see the full effect

8 Reselect the right-click menu on the desktop, and it will now include an entry for the Next desktop background

9 Select this repeatedly to cycle through all the images in the slide show for the theme

By default, the images in the Aero themes slide shows will be exchanged every 30 minutes, but you can adjust this, and also request Shuffle (random image selection), see page 44.

More Themes

1 Select Personalize and then Get more themes online

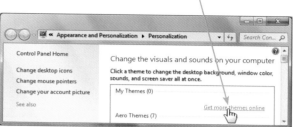

2 The Personalize your PC website offers themes, backgrounds and gadgets (Desktop and SideShow)

3 Scroll down to view the slide show and single image themes offered

Nature

4 When you've found a theme, for example Nature, you'd like to try out, click the Download button below it

42

5 Select to Open the themepack and the file will be downloaded to your computer

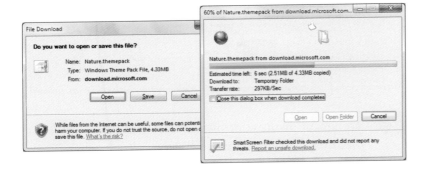

Hot tip

You can also create your own theme by customizing the various components of an existing theme (see page 44).

6 When download completes, the themepack will be installed. Select Allow to confirm this operation

7 Once the themepack is installed, it is activated and added to the My Themes section of Personalization

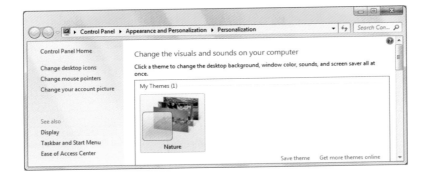

Hot tip

If you want to stop using a theme, select Personalize and choose a different theme. Downloaded themes remain in My Themes until you right-click and select Delete.

43

Customize a Theme

To create your own theme, you start with an existing theme (Windows 7 Theme for example) and change the pictures, colors and sound.

1 Select Personalize, choose the existing theme, then scroll down and select Desktop Background

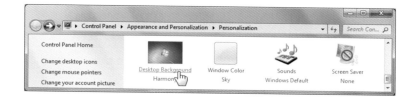

2 To choose from your own library of photos or pictures, click the Browse button

3 Navigate to the folder with your pictures and click OK

4 Choose pictures, then select the delay between picture swaps, and then click Save Changes

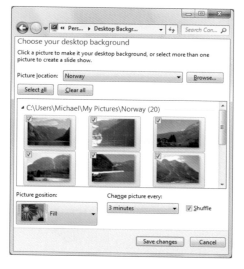

By default all are selected. Hold down the Ctrl key and click pictures to deselect (or click Clear All and select pictures in turn) to have a subset.

You can change the windows color for the selected theme.

1 From Personalization, click Window Color

Window Color
Sky

2 Select the color that should be used for windows borders, Start menu and taskbar

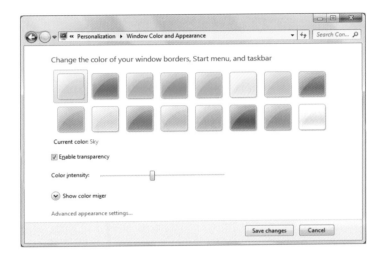

3 Enable or disable transparency and adjust the color intensity slider, then click Save Changes

If you have selected a Basic or a High Contrast theme, or if your computer doesn't support the full Aero capability, the older style Windows Color and Appearance dialog box is displayed.

1 Choose item and color, then click OK to apply change

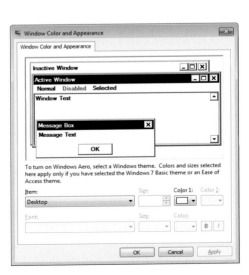

Sounds

You can change the sounds that Windows associates with actions, so you can tell what's happening even if you are not looking at the screen.

1 Select Sounds from Personalization

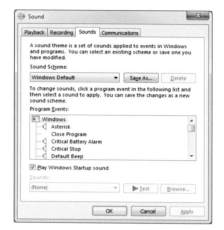

46

2 Click the Sound Scheme bar to select an existing sound scheme, from one of the other Aero themes perhaps

3 To hear the sound that belongs to an action, select the Program Event and then click the Test button

4 When you have modified the scheme, click Save As to keep a named copy

5 Click OK to finish sound for the theme

Screen Saver

You can select a picture or an animation to display while your computer is idle. This is known as a screen saver.

1 Open Personalization and select Screen Saver

2 Click the Screen Saver bar to select from the list, e.g. Photos

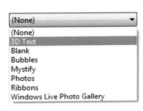

3 This screen saver displays 3D text which spins on the screen, when your computer is idle for one minute

4 Change the delay time, click Settings to adjust the text contents or style, then click OK to apply

Don't forget

Perhaps because of the Slide Show facility, the Screen Saver default is None for the themes.

47

Hot tip

Click the box On resume, display logon screen, if you leave your computer unattended. The password will then be required to carry on using the system.

Save Revised Theme

When you have made changes to a theme, the revised theme will appear under My Themes as an unsaved theme. Color and sound schemes and the screen saver used are identified.

Don't forget

My Themes contains the themes that you have downloaded, customized or installed from shareable themes.

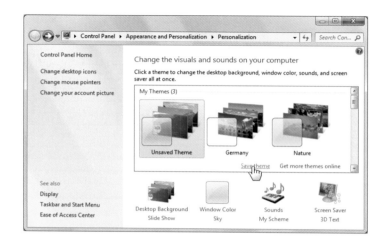

48

1. Select the revised scheme to apply it to the desktop (if not already active) and click Save theme

2. Type a name for your theme and then click Save

3. To let others use your theme, right-click the theme and select Save theme for sharing

4. Enter the name and select Save, and it will be saved in your Documents folder, ready to send to others

Hot tip

Whoever receives a file that's a shareable theme can double-click it to add it to their collection of themes.

Customize Starter Edition

Starter edition does not offer Personalization or Themes, but there are some changes you can make.

1 Click Start and select Appearance and then Display, where you change resolution, screen saver, text size, etc

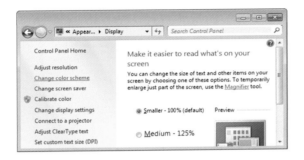

2 Select Change color scheme, and you can change from Windows Basic to Classic or High Contrast

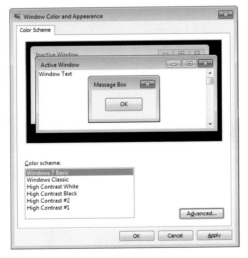

3 Click the Advanced button to select a color for the desktop and to adjust the characteristics of other desktop items

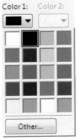

Don't forget

Starter edition has a preset background that can be replaced only by a solid color.

Hot tip

You can make changes only when you select a color scheme other than Windows Basic.

Customize Home Basic

1 Click Start, select Appearance and then Display, where you can change background as well as resolution, screen saver, text size etc

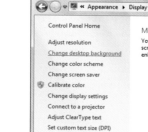

2 Select Change desktop background, and choose one of the images supplied or browse for your own image

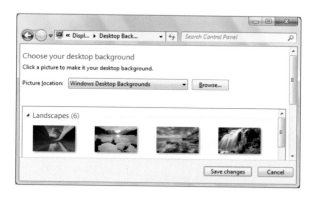

3 Select Change color scheme and you may see an additional option, Windows 7 Standard. This only appears if your computer graphics has Aero capability (even though Home Basic does not include Aero as a feature)

Mouse Settings

Change settings for your mouse to make it easier for you to work with Windows.

1 Select Change mouse pointers from the Personalization dialog

 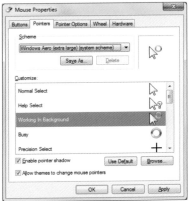

Don't forget

For Starter or Home Basic, click Start, type Mouse, select the Mouse entry and then click the Pointers tab.

2 If you have difficulty spotting the mouse on the display, try an alternative scheme such as Extra Large

3 Click the Pointer Options tab, and you can apply a number of useful changes to help with using the mouse:

Hot tip

For even better visibility, choose the Windows Black (extra large) pointer scheme.

- Change the speed at which the pointer moves

- Automatically place the mouse pointer over the default button, when you switch windows

- Display a trail as you move the pointer, so it is easy to see

- Show the location of the pointer when you press the Ctrl key

...cont'd

Using the mouse can sometimes be a problem for left-handed users. If this applies to you, Windows provides a possible solution.

1   Click the Buttons tab in Mouse Properties

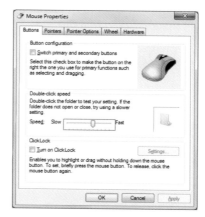

2   Choose to Switch primary and secondary buttons

3   Double-click the folder and if it does not open or close consistently, try a slower setting

4   ClickLock lets you highlight or drag without holding down the mouse button – all that's needed is a brief click to set the click lock

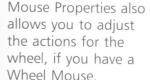
5   Click again to remove the click lock

Screen Resolution

1 Right-click the desktop and select Screen Resolution from the menu

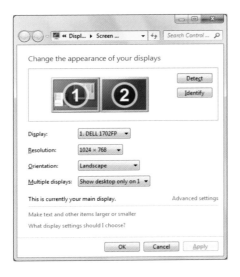

2 Click the Resolution bar and drag the slider to select a new resolution

3 Click the Orientation bar to switch between Landscape and Portrait

Advanced settings

4 Click Advanced settings and select the Monitor tab

5 Click the Screen refresh rate and select a level

6 Click the Apply button to make the changes

Beware

The resolutions and color settings offered depend on the type of monitor and the type of graphics adapter that you have on your computer.

Hot tip

The higher the resolution the more you can fit onto the screen, but the smaller the text and images will appear.

53

Don't forget

Only rates available for the particular resolution will be shown. Higher rates give more comfortable viewing.

Accessibility Options

1 Select Ease of Access Center from the Personalization dialog

2 Alternatively, click Start, Control Panel, Ease of Access then click Ease of Access Center

Hot tip

You'll also find the Ease of Access Center by clicking Start, All Programs, Accessories and then Ease of Access.

3 This opens with a narrator reading the introductory text and listing the main accessibility tools offered

4 Clear the boxes to turn off the narrative on future visits to the Ease of Access Center, if preferred

5 Press the spacebar to start the tool currently highlighted (Magnifier in the illustration above) to see how it might help you

Magnifier

This enlarges a portion of the display in a separate window which follows the mouse pointer. You can also use the whole display for the magnified image.

1 Move the mouse over the spy glass symbol and click to display the Magnifier toolbar

2 Increase or decrease zoom by increments

3 Select View to choose Full screen, Lens or Docked

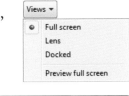

4 Click the Options button to control movement of the Full screen view point

5 Select Options, when in Lens mode, to adjust the size of the Lens window

Get Recommendations

The Ease of Access Center also includes groups of settings to suit various scenarios. Select the ones that may apply to your situation, and it will offer suitable adjustments which will be automatically applied, every time you start Windows.

If you are unsure which options to choose, select the link to Get recommendations to make your computer easier to use. This displays a five-part questionnaire.

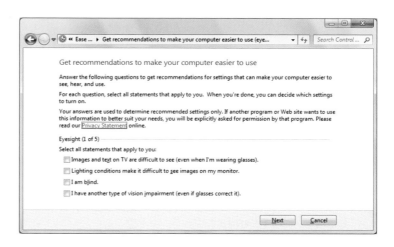

When you have provided your answers, the recommended settings will be displayed ready for you to apply, if desired.

4 Taskbar and Start Menu

Open and switch folder and application windows with Taskbar and Start Menu. Windows Aero adds Flip 3D and live thumbnails. Add shortcuts to Start menu, Taskbar and Jump Lists, and use Windows Touch (if you have a suitable screen).

Taskbar Properties

Hot tip

The Taskbar and its contents, and methods of resizing and locking it, are described on pages 28-29.

To make changes to the Taskbar settings:

1 Select the Taskbar and Start Menu link at the side of the Personalization dialog

2 Alternatively, right-click an empty part of the Taskbar and select Properties from the menu

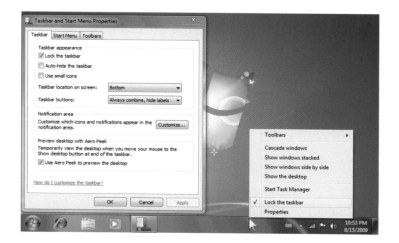

3 You can lock and unlock the Taskbar from Properties as well as from the right-click menu

4 Click the box labelled Auto-hide the Taskbar, to make the full depth of the screen available

 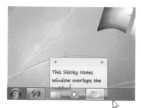

5 It reappears when you move the mouse to the location of the taskbar – the bottom of the screen

...cont'd

Use Small Icons

1 Click the box Use small icons, so you can fit more buttons on the taskbar

Taskbar Location

1 Click the bar labelled Taskbar location on screen, to replace the default Bottom with e.g. Top

Taskbar buttons

The default in Windows 7 is to show taskbar buttons without labels, and to combine windows of the same type. However, you can keep things more separate.

1 Click the bar Taskbar buttons, and select Combine when taskbar is full, to show the task labels

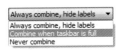

2 Extra tasks may get combined onto the same button

3 With Never combine, taskbar scrolling may be used

Don't forget

There is a separate option to control the Start Menu icon size (see page 69).

Hot tip

There is no need to Unlock the taskbar when you want to change its location on the screen.

59

Don't forget

This style of taskbar works best with higher resolution screens or smaller numbers of active tasks.

Notification Area

In Windows 7, the Notification Area is treated as part of the taskbar. Some icons will appear by default, and when you install programs they may add icons. To control what shows:

1 Click Customize in the Notification Area portion of the Taskbar properties

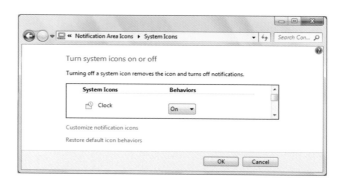

2 Select On for system icons that should always be displayed, or Off for those you want to hide

3 Select Customize notification icons

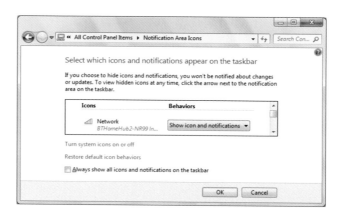

4 For each icon you can choose to Show icon and notification, Hide icon and notification or Only show notification

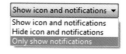

Don't forget

Other system icons include Volume, Action Center, Power (active for Laptop PCs only) and Network (requires some form of network connection).

Don't forget

Icons shown include Network, Action Center and Volume. Icons with Notification only include Windows Update, Windows Explorer and your Antivirus software (in this case AVG).

Show Desktop / Aero Peek

The last item on Taskbar Properties is the option to Preview desktop with Aero Peek. This works in association with the Show Desktop button. Assuming you have a full desktop:

1 Hover over the Show Desktop button to see desktop, icons, gadgets and outlines of all open windows

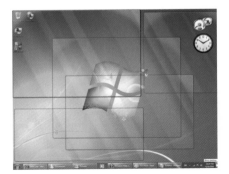

2 Click Show Desktop button to reveal the desktop, click again to restore the desktop

Taskbar Buttons

1 Click Start and open windows, e.g. Welcome Center, Calculator and WordPad, and the taskbar is updated

Hot tip

To open an application, type the first part of the application or folder name in the search box on the Start menu, then select the required item from the results listed.

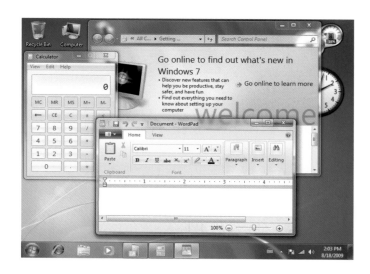

2 When you open more windows, similar windows will be grouped together on the same taskbar button

Don't forget

You can change taskbar properties to get separate taskbar buttons and labels for each of the windows (see page 59).

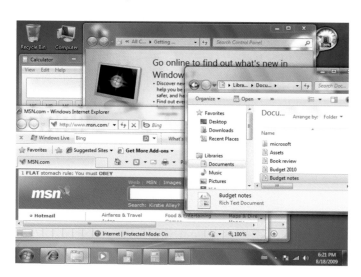

3 This shows there is one Internet Explorer window, two Windows Explorer and at least three WordPad

4 Move the mouse pointer over a taskbar button, and live thumbnails of the window(s) will be displayed

5 Move the pointer over a thumbnail and the window is displayed, with other windows reduced to outlines

63

6 Right-click a thumbnail and the Jump List is displayed, with a list of recently used items, and a link (program name) to open a new instance of the window type

7 There's also an option to unpin or pin to the taskbar

Switching Tasks

When you have a number of windows open, you'll want to be able to switch between tasks. There are numerous ways in which Windows helps you do this efficiently.

 Click any part of a window shown on the desktop, to switch to it and bring it into the foreground

Don't forget

Windows may overlay one another on the screen, so it may be difficult to find the one you want.

Click the Taskbar button for the window you want, to show it (if minimized) and make it the active task

Beware

If there are several tasks on the button, click the button and select the window from the thumbnails (see page 63).

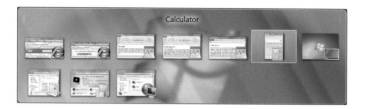

Hold down Alt, press Tab for thumbnails of all tasks, then press Tab until the required task is selected

Press Tab briskly, and all windows stay displayed. Pause a moment after any Tab, and the windows get replaced by outlines, leaving just the window for the current thumbnail. Successive presses of Tab will switch to each window in turn, until you release Alt. This feature is Windows Flip.

Hot tip

Press Alt+Tab, then hold down Alt and press the arrow keys to scroll forward or backward through the window thumbnails.

4 Right-click an empty part of the Taskbar and select
Cascade Windows, and click the window you want

5 To compare two windows, minimize all windows
except those two, then right-click the Taskbar and
select Show windows side by side

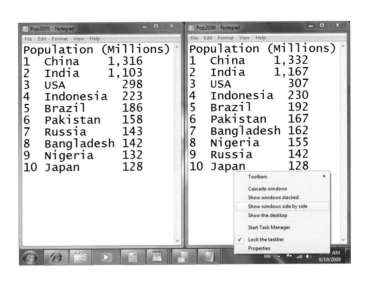

This acts as an alternative to the Snap feature (see page 35).

Don't forget

The Cascade Windows
and Show Windows
options are for visible
windows only, so are
greyed when you have
selected Show the
Desktop or clicked the
Show Desktop button.

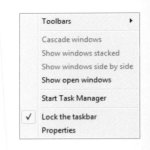

Hot tip

When you select this
option, the Undo
Show side by side
command is added to
the right-click menu.

Aero Flip 3D

With an Aero scheme active, there's a unique way to view and select open windows, which is known as Aero Flip 3D.

Hot tip

All active tasks are displayed, including those minimized to the Taskbar. There's also an entry representing the Desktop itself.

1 Press the Windows Logo key + Tab and you get a large angled view of all windows, with live displays

2 Keep the Windows Logo key depressed and press the Tab key repeatedly to cycle through the windows

Don't forget

The associated live thumbnail(s) appear when you hover the mouse pointer over the task button on the taskbar.

3 Press the Windows Logo key + Ctrl + Tab, and the Aero Flip 3D display stays when you release the keys

4 Press the Tab key to cycle forwards, and press the arrow keys (or roll the mouse wheel) to cycle forwards or backwards

Non-Aero Task Selection

If you have selected a non-Aero theme, or if your system doesn't include Aero support, you'll be running Windows 7 Basic, and the task selection options are more limited.

Hot tip

If you select an Aero theme but turn off transparency (or you have Home Basic with Aero capable hardware) you'll be running Windows 7 Standard. With this, Taskbar and Windows Flip do have live thumbnails, but there is no Aero Flip 3D.

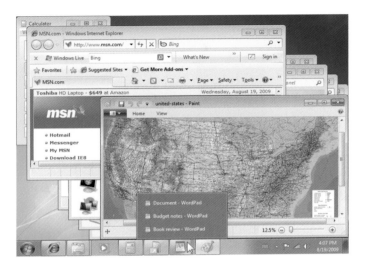

1 Move the mouse pointer over a taskbar button to show the titles of associated documents or windows

2 Press Alt + Tab to display all the tasks as icons, hold down Alt and press Tab until your task appears

Hot tip

Press the Tab key or the arrow keys or roll the mouse wheel, to cycle through the window icons, and press Enter or click the icon when the required task is selected.

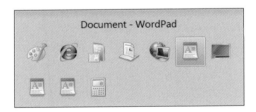

Document - WordPad

3 Press Alt + Ctrl + Tab, and the Windows Flip panel remains displayed when you release the keys.

In this mode, there are no live thumbnails, Aero Flip 3D doesn't operate, and the Windows Logo + Tab key combination does not have any function associated with it.

Start Menu Properties

The Properties dialog used with the Taskbar also controls how the Start menu appears and which entries will be displayed. For example, compared with the default contents (see page 27) this Start menu has:

- Small icons
- Pinned entries at the top
- Computer as a menu
- Fewer entries on the lists

Don't forget

You could also open Taskbar properties (see page 58) and click the Start Menu tab.

Hot tip

Clear the boxes and click Apply, then reselect the boxes, to start afresh with the lists of recently used files and programs.

To make these, and other changes to the Start menu:

1. Right-click the Start button and then select Properties

2. Change the Power button action (see page 36)

3. Clear the boxes in the Privacy section to stop recording recently opened files and programs

4. Click Apply to activate changes

Customize Start Menu

1. Click the Customize button to make changes to actions and appearance

2 Choose Display as Menu to show a list for an entry such as Computer

3 Clear the box to hide entries such as Default Programs

4 Scroll down to review all the entries and options provided

Don't forget

Click OK to exit Customize Start Menu and click Apply or OK, to activate changes.

Other options offered include drag-and-drop menu entries, highlight newly installed programs, open submenus by pausing over them, and set search parameters, as well as more display/no display items. For example, you can:

1 Choose to sort the All Programs menu alphabetically

2 Display the system administrative tools

3 Use small or large icons for programs on the first level of the Start menu

Hot tip

Click the Use Default Settings button to discard all the changes that you have made, now or previously.

Use Default Settings

4 Specify the number of recent programs to display on the Start menu (default is 10)

5 Specify the number of recent items to display in Start menu and Taskbar Jump Lists (default is 10)

Pin Programs

You can pin program shortcuts to the top of the Start menu or to the Taskbar, so that they are always available.

Pin Program to Start Menu

1 Click Start, select All Programs, and navigate to the program you want, then right-click the entry

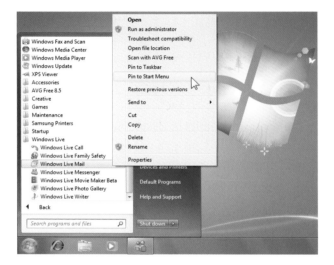

2 Select the option to Pin to Start Menu

3 Select and pin any other programs, e.g. Adobe Reader and XPS Viewer

4 Select Back and you'll see the icons for the selected at the top of the Start menu

Pin Programs to Taskbar:

1 If the program is currently open, right-click the taskbar button to open the program's Jump List

2 Select Pin to Taskbar

3 If the program isn't currently open, click Start, locate the program, right-click and select Pin to Taskbar

The program icon is displayed on the Taskbar, even when the program is closed. Right-click and select Unpin this program from the taskbar, when no longer needed.

You can also pin items in the Jump Lists, so they will always be listed.

Pin Items to Jump List

1 Open the program's Jump List and select the item

2 Click the pushpin icon (or right-click and select Pin to this list

3 The item is added to the Pinned area of the Jump List

4 To remove a pinned item, select it and click the pushpin

Hot tip

You can also drag a program link or shortcut and drop it on the Taskbar.

Don't forget

You can add items or remove items from the Jump List in the Start Menu or on the Taskbar. The two views will be kept the same.

71

Non-Aero Start Menu

With a non-Aero theme, or without Aero-capable hardware, the Start menu changes appearance, though the function remains the same.

Windows Aero

This is the main Windows 7 interface, as used to illustrate the Start menu customization (see page 27).

Windows Standard

This is the style with Transparency disabled (or on a system with the Home Basic edition and with Aero hardware capability).

Windows Basic

You get this interface when you select the Windows 7 Basic theme (or when you have a system with the Starter edition installed).

Windows Classic

This is with the Windows Classic theme selected. This can be enabled in any edition of Windows 7.

High Contrast White

The remaining interfaces are the four high contrast themes, which are provided in all the Windows 7 editions, to give improved visibility.

Hot tip

In Windows Vista, you could select the Classic Start menu, with the old style of previous versions of Windows. This is not offered in Windows 7.

Windows Touch

Your normal choices are mouse or keyboard, to manage windows, operate the taskbar and interact with applications. With the right hardware, however, there is another option – you can touch the screen to indicate your wishes, taking advantage of the Windows touch capabilities.

To use this feature, you'll need a display that supports touch, such as the Asus Eee Top ET2002/ET2203 series.

These are all-in-one computers with either 20" or 21.6" HD display sizes, and feature a touch-screen interface supported by Windows 7 Home Premium. They also include Bluetooth and Wi-Fi so they can have Internet connection and be used anywhere in the home.

In Windows 7 you can drag your finger across taskbar thumbnail previews and trigger a peek at the associated window. A tap will select that window. Similarly, the Show Desktop button supports press-and-hold to reveal your desktop, while a tap will clear the desktop.

With Windows Explorer, you can zoom in on an image by moving two fingers closer together, or zoom out by moving two fingers apart. This, for example, allows you to switch between Small icon and Extra Large icon views.

The onscreen keyboard also supports touch, so you can tap key images to enter keystrokes. Multitouch support means you can press multiple buttons at the same time, allowing you, for example, to capitalize letters.

If you touch an icon with one finger and tap with another, this is treated just like pressing the right mouse button for that icon, and Windows will display the appropriate context menu. From this you can select by tapping an entry.

Tablet PCs

There is a set of Windows touch gestures that provide the basic actions you need to interact with Windows or an application using touch. These gestures are designed to work with all applications, even if they were not specifically designed for touch operations.

GESTURE	WINDOWS USAGE	GESTURE ACTION	ACTION (○ = finger down | ○ = finger up)	Single Touch	Windows Touch
Tap / Double Tap	Click / Double Click			✦	✦
Panning with Inertia	Scrolling	Drag 1 or 2 fingers up and down			✦
Selection / Drag (left to right with one finger)	Mouse Drag / Selection	Drag one finger left / right		✦	✦
Press and Tap	Right-click	Press on target and tap using a second finger			✦
Zoom	Zoom (defaults to Control Scroll wheel)	Move two fingers apart / toward each other			✦
Rotate	No system default unless handled by Application (using WM_GESTURE API)	Move two fingers in opposing directions -or- Use one finger to pivot around another			✦
Two-Finger Tap	N/A – Exposed through Gesture API, used by Application discretion.	Tap two fingers at the same time (where the target is the midpoint between the fingers)			✦
Press and Hold	Right-click	Press, wait for blue ring animation to complete, then release		✦	✦
Flicks	Default: Pan up/ Pan Down/ Back, and Forward	Make quick drag gestures in the desired direction		✦	✦

Tablet PC

With a Tablet PC, the screen twists and folds away to present you with a surface where you get handwriting and formula recognition when you write, in addition to the Windows Touch capabilities. For example, Asus Eee PC T91MT is a netbook with Windows 7 Home Premium edition and supports multitouch gesture and multitouch command.

5 Gadgets and Devices

Desktop Gadgets are small applications that offer useful functions and information. Hardware devices such as USB flash drives can be used to boost performance. Use SideShow gadgets if your computer has a supplementary display. Add devices such as network printers.

Desktop Gadgets

Desktop Gadgets provide another way to run tasks. Gadgets are small, easy-to-use and customizable mini-applications. There's a collection of gadgets included in Windows, though they need to be explicitly enabled, since there are no gadgets included with the default configuration. To see what's available and to start gadgets:

1 Right-click the desktop and select Gadgets from the menu

2 Double-click any gadget to add it to the desktop, on the right hand side

Don't forget

In Vista, gadgets were stored on the Sidebar, an area at the right on the desktop. Gadgets can appear anywhere on the desktop in Windows 7, though initially they are placed in the area previously used by the Sidebar.

76

3 Click the arrow to switch to the second page of the gallery

4 Click Show details for the selected gadget

Managing Gadgets

Point to any one of the gadgets and several buttons appear on the right.

1 Click the Close button to remove that gadget from the Sidebar (it will stay in the local Gadget Gallery)

2 Click the Size button to view a larger version with more details

3 Click the Options button to adjust settings

Options offered are specific to the particular gadget. With the Weather gadget, you search for the location that you want to track. You can also choose to display temperatures in Fahrenheit or Centigrade.

Hot tip

Add a second copy of the Clock gadget and you can display the time from two different zones.

For the Clock gadget, you can choose the appearance from a selection of 8 styles, assign a name, specify the time zone to be displayed, and show or hide the second hand.

You can also right-click an open gadget to select Add gadgets, Move, Size, Always on Top, Opacity, Options or Close gadget.

Don't forget

If you choose Always on top, select a level of opacity below 100%, to make the gadget less intrusive.

Arranging Gadgets

To reposition the open gadgets:

1 Click the Drag gadget button and move the gadget to any position on the monitor

If you have gadgets hidden under windows:

2 Use Show Desktop or Aero Peek (see page 61) to locate the open gadgets

(see page 61)

 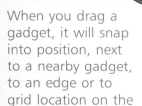

3 Press the Windows Logo key + G, to bring the gadgets to the front of the desktop

4 If you have dual monitors on your computer, you can choose to put gadgets on either display

Get More Gadgets

Windows 7 provides a basic set of gadgets, but you can download more gadgets from the online Gadget Gallery.

1 Right-click the desktop and select Gadgets to open the Desktop Gadget Gallery

2 Click the link Get more gadgets online

3 For more choice, click Get more desktop gadgets

4 Review by category, or type keywords and click Gallery

Hot tip

This opens the same Personalize your PC web page that you see when you look for new Aero themes (see page 42) but with the Desktop Gadgets tab selected.

Beware

Many of these gadgets will have been optimized for Windows Vista. However, they should still operate under Windows 7.

Download Gadget

You can put gadgets from the Internet into your Desktop
Gadget Gallery. To download a gadget:

1 Search the online galleries to find gadgets you want

2 Click Download
for the gadget

3 Click Install to
confirm request

4 Follow the prompts to download the
gadget and add it to desktop and gallery

Beware

If you Close the new
gadget, it will remain
in the gallery until you
right-click it there and
select Uninstall.

Install New Device

Most devices can be installed by plugging them into your computer. Windows will add the required driver software if it is available (or prompt you for the CD that came with the hardware).

To install a USB device, such as a flash drive or a portable hard drive, onto your computer:

1 Insert the device into one of your USB ports

2 Windows identifies the device and begins installing the driver software required

3 Installation completes and the device is ready to use

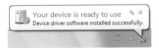

4 The AutoPlay dialog will offer you options that are appropriate to the contents of the USB device, which in this case has music and photos

5 Click Open folder to view files and folders, if no specific action is needed

Beware

Your particular device may require you to install the software before plugging in the hardware. Always check the instructions before you start the installation.

Don't forget

The options offered on the AutoPlay dialog will differ, depending on the file types of the contents, and the device characteristics (see page 83).

Hot tip

The next time you attach this device, the AutoPlay dialog displays immediately, since installation is already completed.

Safely Remove Hardware

When you've finished working with the USB storage device, you should make sure that the computer has finished saving any information before you unplug the device.

Beware

Removing the device without checking that data transfer has completed could be damaging for both data content and device.

1 Wait until the activity light stops flashing

2 Locate the Safely Remove Hardware icon in the notification area, click this and select the device

3 Unplug the device when you are told it is safe to remove hardware

If the device is classified as removable, you can also initiate disconnection via the Computer folder.

Don't forget

USB flash drives will generally be classed as removable, but USB portable drives are normally treated as hard disks.

1 Select Start, Computer then right-click the entry for the drive

2 Select Eject, then unplug the device when notified that it is safe to do so

ReadyBoost

Windows can use the storage space on most flash USB drives and flash memory cards to speed up your computer. The AutoPlay dialog offers this as an option when you insert the device.

1. Choose the option Speed up my system

2. Select Dedicate this device to ReadyBoost

3. Windows recommends how much to reserve for system speed

4. To stop using the space, open the device properties and choose Do not use this device

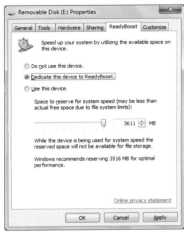

Not all USB storage devices are capable of being used for this purpose. The drive is tested the first time it is inserted, and the results may show that it is unsuitable.

Testing is switched off and the ReadyBoost option will not be offered in AutoPlay, the next time this drive is inserted.

Windows SideShow

Windows SideShow is the feature in Windows 7 that supports an auxiliary display. This could be specified as part of a notebook, desktop computer or as a separate device.

On the auxiliary display, you can work with information, such as emails, calendar data, media player status and weather updates, without having to run the main computer.

To see SideShow in action, you need to have a SideShow-compatible device running. If you want to explore the concept without committing to the hardware, Microsoft has a SideShow simulator that mimics a SideShow device, so you can see how SideShow works.

1 Attach your SideShow device application (or start the SideShow Device Simulator)

The SideShow simulator comes in three guises – Touch, Landscape and Portrait – and has several gadgets included.

Hot tip

There are SideShow compatible devices such as MP3 players, remote controls and mobile phones that can act as auxiliary displays and run SideShow Gadgets.

Don't forget

To find the SideShow simulator, go to the www.microsoft.com/downloads website and search for Device Simulator SideShow. Download the setup software and follow the prompts to install.

To specify additional SideShow gadgets or change settings:

1 Select SideShow from Hardware and Sounds in the Control Panel

2 Click the box to turn on any gadget listed, or select Get more gadgets online to add more programs

3 Click Download to install individual gadgets

The gadgets you select are added to SideShow in Control Panel, ready to be turned on for the SideShow device.

Install Printers

Hot tip

When you directly connect a printer to your computer, Windows will normally detect it and add it to the system configuration.

1 Connect a USB printer such as the Lexmark Z51

2 Windows detects the printer and starts installing the device driver software

Configuration and setup tasks may be carried out. For example, you may be asked to specify the inkjet cartridge types and run a cartridge alignment print.

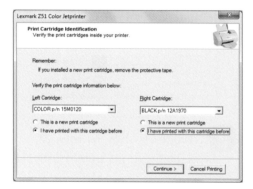

3 The device driver installation is completed

4 You'll now find the printer in Devices and Printers

Don't forget

If this is the first physical printer added (i.e. excluding software printers such as Fax and XPS) it will be made the default printer (as shown by the tick mark).

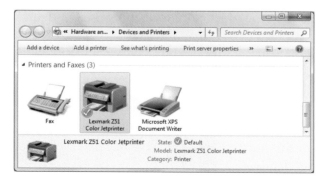

If Windows does not recognize the device, or is not able to install a suitable driver, you get a warning message:

Windows may provide a link to the manufacturer's website, where you can find a suitable driver.

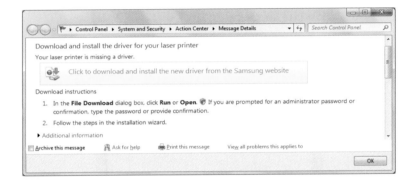

① Download and run the recommended driver software for your printer

② The new printer is added to the Devices and Printers folder, as the new default printer

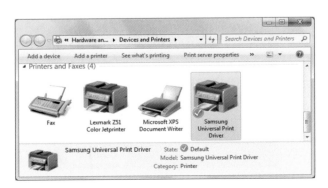

Access Network Printer

You may need to start with the installation CD to set up a printer on your system, whether local or network connected. For example, to access an existing wireless printer:

1 Insert the Installation CD for the printer, and select the setup program from AutoPlay

2 Follow the prompts until asked if you are setting up a new printer

3 Choose No, to add an existing networked printer

4 Choose the connection type – wireless (as in this example), wired or USB cable direct attachment

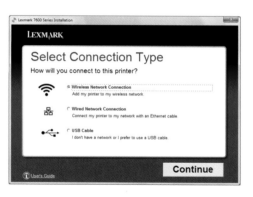

5 Select your printer by name from the printer or printers displayed for your wireless network

6 When the printer is prepared, print a sample page

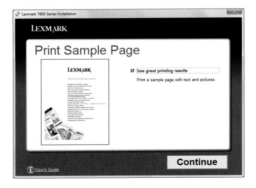

7 The printer is added to Devices and Printers

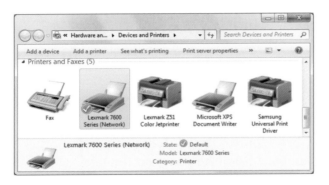

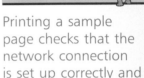

Don't forget

Printing a sample page checks that the network connection is set up correctly and the printer can handle text and graphics across the network.

Hot tip

The wireless printer is set as the default so again you'll need to amend this if appropriate.

Control Panel

The Control Panel allows you to change settings for the hardware and software components in Windows.

1 Click the Start button and select Control Panel

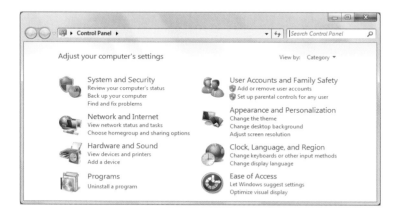

2 Select any category to explore Control Panel contents, for example click User Accounts and Family Safety

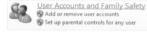

3 Select a subcategory such as User Accounts, or a related task such as Change your Windows password

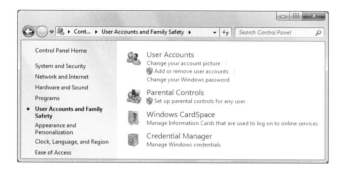

4 Click Control Panel Home or select another category from the panel on the left

...cont'd

You can search the Control Panel for settings or tasks.

1 Type a word or phrase in the search box, for example type the word User

2 All subcategories and tasks related to the search terms will be listed

3 You can also search Help and Support

Don't forget

When you search from the Start menu, entries found in the Control Panel are also displayed.

Another way to browse the Control Panel is to view the contents by icons.

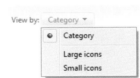

1 Click the View by box, and select Large or Small Icons

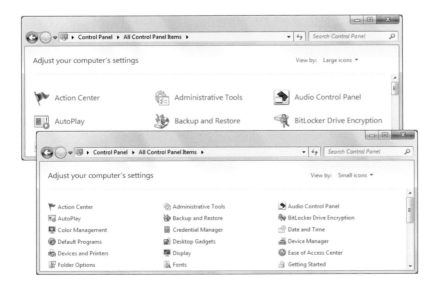

Hot tip

Type the initial letter of the item name to select the first item beginning with that letter. You can also use the Search field (as shown above for Category view).

2 Use the arrow keys to scroll through the list of icons

Regional Settings

Hot tip

To illustrate the use of the Control Panel, you can make changes to the regional settings on your computer.

Don't forget

You can define additional taskbar clocks to show the time in other zones.

1 Select the Clock, Language and Region category

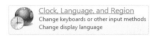

Clock, Language, and Region
Change keyboards or other input methods
Change display language

2 Select Date and Time to adjust time or change the time zone

3 Click Internet Time to reset the time using an online clock

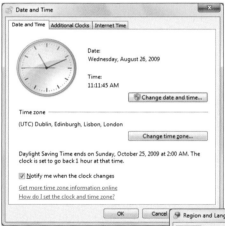

4 Select Regional and Language to view or change the date format, the location and the languages specified for input and for display

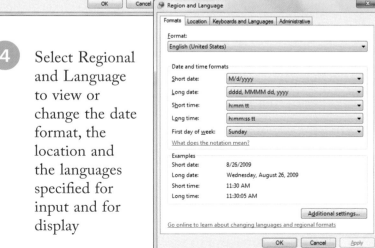

6 Search and Organize

Windows 7 helps organize the files and folders on your hard disk. Data is stored by username with separate folders for different types of files, or you can add new folders. Libraries allow you to work with a group of folders. Powerful instant search facilities help you find your way around the folders and the menus.

Files and Folders

The hardware components are the building blocks for your computer but it is the information on your disk drive that really makes your computer operate. There is a huge number of files and folders stored there. To get an idea of how many:

1 Click the Start button and select Computer, then select the system disk, e.g. the C: drive

Local Disk (C:)
62.0 GB free of 80.1 GB

2 Double-click the drive to open it

Hot tip

Alternatively, you could open the drive, click Organize, Select All and then click Organize, Properties.

3 Press Ctrl+A to select all the items

4 Right-click the selection and click Properties

94

Hot tip

This shows some of the hidden folders on the system hard disk

5 This shows that the system has more than 55,000 files and nearly 10,000 folders

6 There are actually even more files and folders stored on the disk, hidden and system files. These are hidden to protect them from inadvertant changes

With so many files and folders to deal with, they must be well organized to ensure that you can locate the documents, pictures and other data that you require. Windows helps by organizing the files into related sections, for example:

- Program Files   Application programs
- Temp   Temporary system and program files
- Windows   Operating system programs and data
- Users   Documents, pictures, etc.

These are the top-level folders on your hard disk and each of them is divided into subfolders. For example, the Program Files folder is arranged by supplier and application.

1   Open the C: drive, then double-click Program Files, then Adobe and then the subfolder Reader

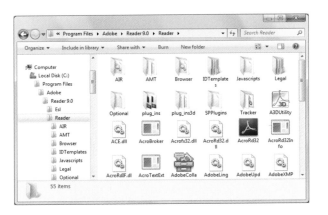

2   Move the mouse pointer over the navigation pane and you'll see triangles associated with some folders

3   The white triangle (▷) shows there are subfolders within, and the black triangle (◢) means an expanded folder

Hot tip

The Users folder contains Document, Pictures, Music and other folders listed on the Start menu (see page 27).

Don't forget

The Program Files and Windows folders are managed by the system, and you will not normally need to access them directly.

Hot tip

The triangle symbols also appear when you select any of the folder names within the navigation pane.

New User Account

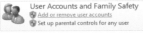

1 Select Start, Control Panel and in User Accounts and Family Safety click Add or remove user accounts

2 Click the option to Create a new account

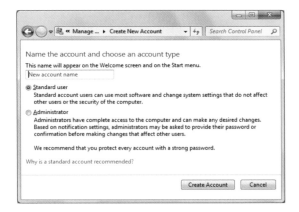

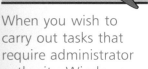
3 Specify the account name and choose the account type

It is recommended to create a standard user account for every user, including the administrator, to minimize the risk of unintended changes.

4 Click the Create Account button

The Manage Accounts dialog will be displayed. You can now add a password to the new account or make other changes.

1 Select the account that you want to change

You can change the picture associated with the account, for example by selecting a user photograph.

2 Select the change, for example Create a password

3 Type a password, then re-enter it to confirm

You are recommended to use a strong password. This should be at least eight characters, with mixed upper case, lower case, numbers and symbols, avoiding words and names.

4 Type a password hint if desired, then click Create Password

Each account will have its own set of files and folders, and also personal preferences such as color theme or desktop background.

User Folders

Don't forget

Public is available to all user accounts, and can be used to share files with other people using the same computer or using other computers on the same network.

The documents and pictures that you create or save on your computer are stored in folders associated with your user name. To explore these:

1 Open the C: drive and double-click the icon for the Users folder

2 There's a folder for each user account name defined, plus the Public folder

3 Double-click the folder for the active user account, i.e. Michael

There's a set of subfolders with all the documents, pictures and settings belonging to that user.

Each user folder (including the Public folder) has a similar set of subfolders defined.

Some of the user subfolders can also be accessed from the Libraries in Navigation pane.

Hot tip

To see the hierarchical structure of the user folders, right-click the Navigation pane and select Expand to current folder.

Show all folders
✓ Expand to current folder

4 Expand the Libraries entry by clicking the white triangle (▷) and you'll see links to the Documents, Music, Pictures and Videos libraries.

Libraries

Libraries in Windows 7 provide a place where you can manage your documents, music, pictures and other files. There are four default libraries – Documents, Music, Pictures and Videos – which allow you to access the associated folders for the current user and for Public. To see the libraries:

1 Click the Libraries entry in the Navigation pane for any folder window, Computer for example

Hot tip

To display the libraries using the Start menu search, select Start, type libraries and then press Enter.

2 Double-click the Pictures library to open it

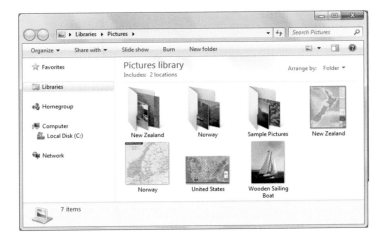

Don't forget

The libraries have links to all the files and subfolders in the locations defined for that library, but the actual files and subfolders remain where they were originally stored.

3 By default, the library is shown in Folder view, with all the files and subfolders in two locations – My Documents and Public Documents

Add Folder to Library

1 Attach the device, if the folder is on a separate drive, open Computer and double-click the drive icon

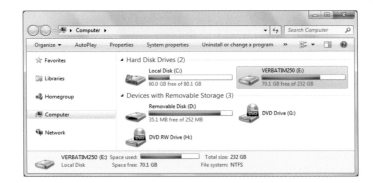

2 Select the required folder and click Include in library, then select the appropriate library, e.g. Pictures

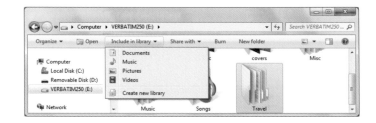

3 The folder and subfolders are added to the library as an additional location, and folders grouped by name

...cont'd

To display the contents of a library in a different arrangement:

1 Open the library, click the box next to Arrange by and select an option, for example Month

2 The files in the library folders are re-organized by month of file creation (e.g. date photos imported)

3 Double-click one of the stacks, for example January 2009, and the files are displayed (by day, newest first)

The files that are grouped together may come from any of the folders or subfolders in the library, even if they are on different drives.

Hot tip

The attributes displayed for the Arrange by function depend on the library type. For Documents or Music you'd choose from:

Don't forget

The icon for each of the monthly groups is created from a selection of the files in that group, set in a stack formation.

Working with Libraries

Although the files in the library collection are stored in different folders or drives, you can work with them as though they are in the same folder. For example:

1 From a group of Picture library items, make a selection and click Preview to see them enlarged

2 Similarly, select Slide show to view the items as a full screen slide show, or click Print to send them to the printer, or click Burn to write them to disc

Folder Navigation

When you open a drive or folder, you'll find a number of different ways to navigate among the folders on your disk.

1 Open the Documents folder on the Start menu

Address bar · Contents pane · Search box

Forward and Back buttons

Libraries

Navigation pane

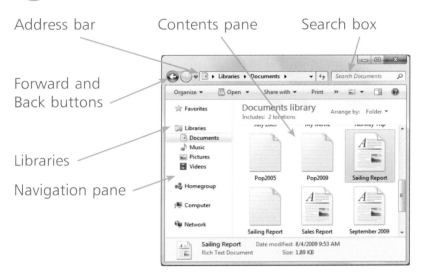

Hot tip

Click the Forward and Back buttons to navigate through locations you have already visited.

Don't forget

The address bar displays the current location as a series of links, separated by arrows.

2 To go directly to a location on the Address bar, just click that location, for example the User folder (in this case Michael)

3 To go to a subfolder of a location on the Address bar, click the arrow at the right, and select a subfolder from the list

4 To type a location, click the blank space to the right of the current location to display the current folder address

5 Edit the folder address for the required location, e.g. C:\Users\Public\Documents and then press Enter

Hot tip

For common locations, you can type just the name, for example:
- Computer
- Contacts
- Control Panel
- Documents
- Pictures

Create Folders and Files

Create new folders to organize your documents.

1 Open the library or folder where the new folder is required, for example select Start, Documents

2 Right-click an empty part of the folder area and select New Folder (or choose a particular file type)

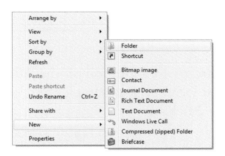

Choose one of the file types, for example Rich Text Document, and it will be initially named as New Rich Text Document. Overtype this name, as shown for the new folder.

3 Overtype the name New Folder with the required name and press Enter (or click elsewhere)

If you create a folder or a file in a library such as Documents or Pictures, it will be created and stored within the library's default save location, for example the current user's My Documents or My Pictures.

Copy or Move Files

You can copy a file using the Windows clipboard.

1 Open the folder containing the file, right-click the
file icon and select Copy (to record the file path)

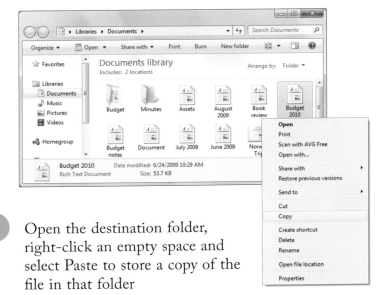

Hot tip

You could also select
the file, and then click
Organize, Copy. The
keyboard shortcut for
this is Ctrl+C.

2 Open the destination folder,
right-click an empty space and
select Paste to store a copy of the
file in that folder

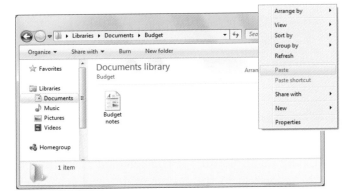

Hot tip

Alternatively, select the
folder and then click
Organize, Paste. The
keyboard shortcut for
this is Ctrl+V.

3 To move the file rather than make a
copy, you'd right-click and choose Cut

4 The original file icon will be dimmed until
you select Paste, when it will be transferred
to the new location

Hot tip

The equivalent options
are Organize, Cut and
the keystroke Ctrl+X.

...cont'd

To move or copy files using drag-and-drop operations:

1 Open the folder with the files you want to move

2 Select the first file then press the Ctrl key as you select the second and subsequent files

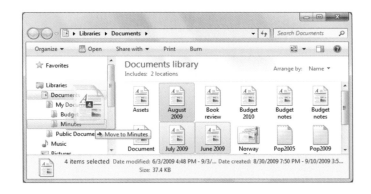

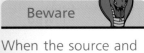

Copy here
Move here
Create shortcuts here

Cancel

3 Click and hold any of the selected files, then drag the selection to the target folder and release there

4 To Copy rather than Move the files, hold down Ctrl as you drag and release the selection

5 If the target folder is in a different drive, hold down Shift as you drag to Move, otherwise you will Copy

Delete Files

To remove files from a folder:

1 Select the file or files, right-click the selection and click Delete (or select Organize, Delete)

2 You'll be asked if you are sure

3 Click Yes to confirm

4 Files on the hard disk will be moved to the Recycle bin (files on other drives are removed immediately)

To recover a file deleted by mistake:

1 Right-click the Recycle bin and select Open, or simply double-click the icon

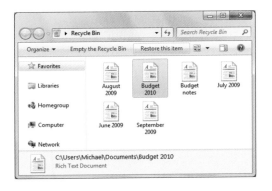

2 Select the file required and click Restore this item

3 Click Empty the Recycle Bin to remove files from the hard disk permanently and free up disk space

Hot tip

Pressing the keyboard Delete key will have the same effect as selecting the Delete menu entry.

Don't forget

To remove hard disk files completely without using the Recycle bin as an interim store, hold down Shift as you select Delete.

Beware

If the Recycle bin doesn't appear, see page 30 to show desktop icons.

Folder Views

The Change your View button on the folder toolbar cycles through a set of five different views of the folder contents.

1 Open a library or folder, for example Documents, and note the file list style in use (i.e. Large Icons)

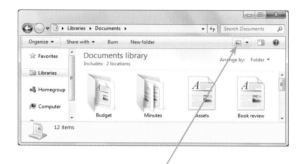

2 Click Change your View button and it changes to the List view

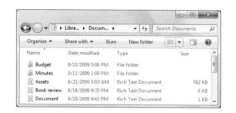

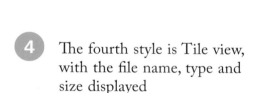
3 Click again to get the Details view

4 The fourth style is Tile view, with the file name, type and size displayed

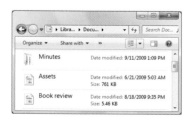

5 The last style offered is the Content view with details based on file type

Pressing the Views button again returns to Large Icons view.

There are additional views available, but these must be explicitly selected

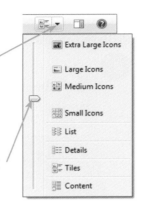

1. Click the arrow next to the Views button and the full list is shown, including Extra Large, Medium and Small Icons views

2. Select the required style, or drag the slider between Extra Large and Small to pick a custom size

The icons are based on the file type, except for image files, which use a miniature thumbnail of the actual contents. For example, this is the Pictures library with Extra Large Icons:

Don't forget

A file type icon rather than a thumbnail is used for the Small Icons, List and Details views.

For Library folders, Arrange By provides a special view that stacks the images by the file creation month (see page 101).

Folder Layout

You can control which parts of the library or folder are displayed in the folder window:

 Open the Pictures library in the typical layout, with the Library, Navigation and Details panes displayed, and, in this case, with the contents shown in List view

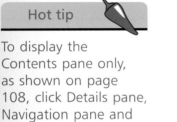

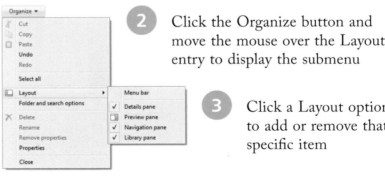

 Click the Organize button and move the mouse over the Layout entry to display the submenu

 Click a Layout option to add or remove that specific item

An icon indicates that the particular item is hidden, and the Tick symbol shows you have selected an item.

 For example, select Menu Bar and Preview Pane in turn, to display these on the folder

...cont'd

This shows all the elements for a library folder, including the Menu Bar familiar in previous releases of Windows.

Click the Show the Preview Pane button on the toolbar to display or hide the Preview Pane without having to select the Layout submenu.

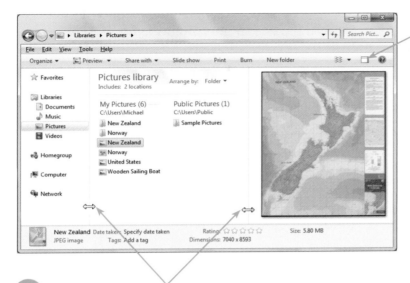

1 To change the pane sizes, move the mouse pointer over the line separator, and drag using the resize arrow, or resize the whole window (see page 34)

(see page 34)

Hot tip

The preview image is automatically resized to make full use of the preview pane, while retaining the image proportions.

111

When you open a folder rather than a library, there is no Library pane, and the associated entry is removed from the Organize, Layout submenu.

Don't forget

If you select a Notepad or WordPad file, the text contents are shown in the Preview pane. For other file types, you may see the message No preview available.

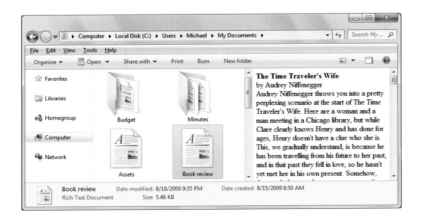

Search Box

If you want to find a file, but are not sure which subfolder it is in, you can start at the higher-level folder and use the Search box to find the exact location.

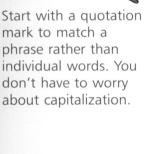
1 Open the Music library from the Start menu

2 Click the Search box and start typing the search words, e.g. "love is all around"

3 As you type, matches so far are listed in the Search Results folder

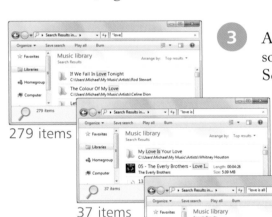

279 items

37 items

8 items

4 items

4 Stop typing when the results show the file you are seeking or when the window shows the whole list

Start Menu Search

If you don't have a starting point, or if the files you want are spread across several locations, then use Start Menu Search.

1 Click the Start button and type your search word(s), e.g. documents

2 The count and first few results by category (e.g. Programs, Control Panel, Documents and Files) are listed

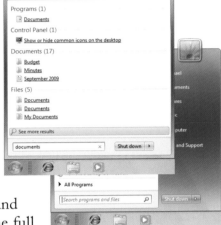

3 Click See more results to open the Search Folder and see the details of the full list of matches

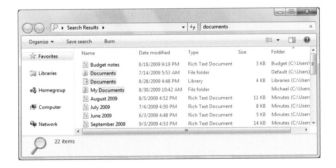

4 The results are sorted by folder name, but you can click any of the file list headers to resequence the list

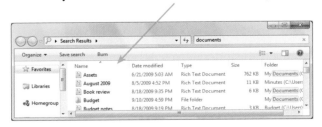

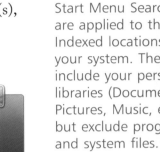

Don't forget

Start Menu Searches are applied to the Indexed locations on your system. These include your personal libraries (Documents, Pictures, Music, etc.), but exclude program and system files.

Hot tip

Click the header a second time, to sort the list in the reverse sequence.

Search Index

Windows uses the Search Index to perform fast searches of the most common files on your computer, scanning the index instead of examining the files.

If you are searching in locations that are not indexed, the search may be very slow because Windows has to examine every file in those locations.

1 Open Control Panel, type Indexing in the Search box and select Indexing Options

2 The locations currently indexed are displayed

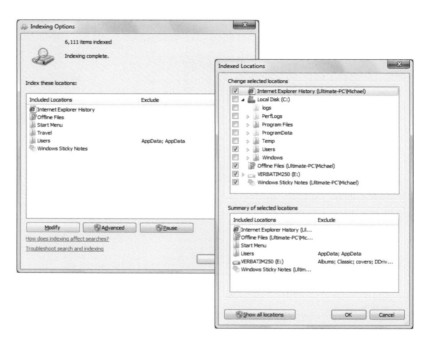

When you include a folder in one of your libraries, it is automatically added to the index.

3 Click Modify to add or remove specific folders

As with libraries, you cannot add folders that are stored on removable devices such as CD, DVD or USB flash drives. Also, if you've indexed an external device such as a USB drive, you'll see it marked as unavailable if it is disconnected when you open Indexing Options.

...cont'd

To add or remove file types or adjust settings:

1 Open Indexing Options, click the Advanced button, and select the File Types tab

2 Select a file type to see how it is indexed

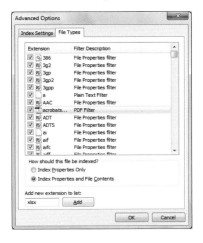

Most file types are indexed by properties only, but file types containing text are normally indexed by both properties and contents.

3 Type a file extension that's not yet included and click Add

4 Choose how to index that particular file type, then click OK to apply the changes

Beware

With any location, you can click the box to include non-indexed and system files, but the search may take much longer.

To adjust index settings:

1 Click the Index Settings tab

2 Include encrypted files in the index

3 If there are problems finding files that should be indexed, click Rebuild to recreate the index

Don't forget

Encrypting File System (EFS) is only included in Windows 7 Enterprise, Professional and Ultimate editions.

4 You can choose where to store the index, but you should make sure it is on a non-removable drive

Like Rebuild, this recreates the index which takes time.

Folder and Search Options

Don't forget

The Organize menu also allows you to control the operation of folders and search tools.

Hot tip

You can adjust the current folder (file list view, panes, etc) and apply the changes to all your folders.

1 From an open folder, click Organize and select Folder and Search Options

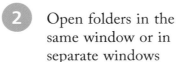

2 Open folders in the same window or in separate windows

3 Open items with Single-click or double-click

4 Show all folders on the Navigation pane

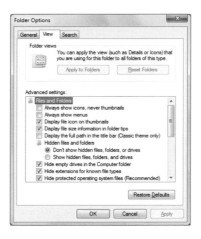

5 Choose advanced settings such as Always show icons, never thumbnails or Show hidden files and folders

6 Clear the box Hide extensions for known file types to reveal file extensions in file names

7 For non-indexed locations, say whether to search contents as well as file names

8 Include subfolders, use natural language or search in compressed files, as preferred

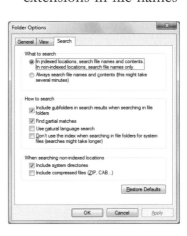

7 Email and Calendar

Windows Live Mail provides the functions needed for secure and effective email communications. It also provides Contacts for the necessary address book functions and Calendar to keep track of events and meetings. You can also communicate via Instant Messaging, Webmail and online Newsgroups.

Electronic Mail

Don't forget

An email address consists of a user name or nickname, the @ sign, and the server name of your email provider, e.g. jsmith99@myisp.com.

Email or electronic mail is used to send and receive text messages. You can send an email message to anyone with an email address, you can receive messages from anyone who knows your email address and you can reply to those messages, or forward them to another email address. You can send your email message to more than one person at the same time, and attach files such as documents or pictures.

Email is free, since no stamp or fee is required. However, before you can use email, you require:

- An account with an Internet Service Provider (ISP)
- An Internet connection such as telephone or cable
- A modem or router to make the connection
- An email address from your email service provider
- An email program such as Windows Live Mail

Hot tip

You can also send and receive email using your web browser, if the email account you use supports webmail (see page 130).

Windows Live Mail is one of the Windows Live Essentials (see page 37). It provides Windows 7 with an equivalent to the Windows Mail and Outlook Express applications found in previous releases of Windows. In addition to email, it also supports newsgroups. These are Internet-based discussion forums where members share information and opinions on topics of mutual interest. Windows Live Mail helps you read the messages posted by other members, and add your own messages to the forum for others to read.

To set up Windows Live Mail to use your email account you'll need the following information:

Don't forget

These details should be given to you by your email service provider. In some cases, the provider may update your Windows Live Mail settings automatically, so you don't have to enter the details.

- Display name (appears at the top of email messages)
- Email address (created when you initially signed up)
- Server names (incoming and outgoing email servers)
- Server type (usually POP3 or IMAP)
- Password (also created when you signed up)

Windows Live Mail

To add an email account to Windows Live Mail:

1 Click the Start button, then click the E-mail entry near the top of the Start menu

2 Windows Live Mail starts up and (if there's no email account already defined) it automatically prompts you for the details

3 Enter your full email address (the account name and the server address, separated by the @ symbol)

4 Type the name as you'd like it to appear in the From field in your email messages

5 Windows can usually add the server details for the specific ISP, or you can choose to add them manually

6 Click Next to continue

Don't forget

You need to be connected to the Internet (see page 136) to complete this operation. In this example there is an existing DSL connection.

Beware

You must enter this address exactly as given, without spaces or changing capitalization.

119

Hot tip

If you leave this entry blank, your email address will be used for the From field.

...cont'd

Don't forget

The specifications for the email servers are dependent on the particular service, but the details shown are typical.

Beware

You must click the box if you have been told that your outgoing server will require authentication.

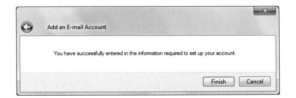

Hot tip

The easiest way to test the setup is to send a message to yourself.

7 Specify incoming server type (POP3 or IMAP) and name, and outgoing server name, then click Next

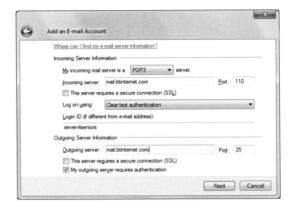

8 Click Finish, and your account will be set up

9 Click New to create a message (see page 126) to test your account

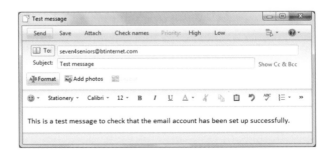

10 Click Send to send the message

Layout

1 Open Windows Live Mail and, if prompted, make this your default email program

2 Your test message appears, along with any other messages that may be awaiting you

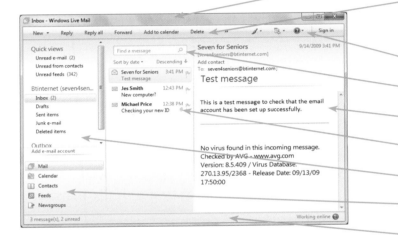

Title bar

Command bar

Toolbar

Search box

Reading pane

Attachment icon

Folder list

Shortcuts

Status bar

To avoid previewing messages:

1 Click the Menus button and select Layout

2 Clear the box labeled Show the reading pane

3 Amend other sections of the windows, and click Apply

Layout...

Options...
Safety options...

Customize toolbar...

Show menu bar

Hot tip

Hiding the Reading pane will reduce the chance of inadvertently opening messages that are spam.

Don't forget

Select Folder pane to use compact shortcuts, turn off the Quick Views, etc.

Receive Mail

You can check to see if there is any mail waiting for you on the incoming mail server.

1 In Windows Live Mail, to check immediately for mail, click the Sync button

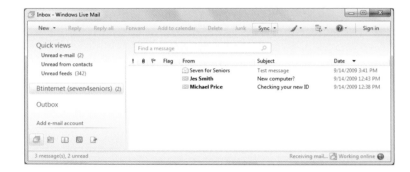

2 Windows Live Mail connects to the Internet (if not already connected) and initiates retrieval of email

3 Click the Mail icon for details of the transfer

4 The messages are added to your Inbox, latest first (click the Received header to sort in reverse order)

View Message

1 Double-click an entry in the Inbox list to open the message (or select the entry and press Enter)

Hot tip

A highlighted entry is one that has not yet been read. The number in brackets after Inbox in the Folders list indicates how many such messages there are.

2 The message opens in a new window

3 To respond, click the Reply button on the toolbar

Don't forget

Click Reply All to respond to everyone who received the original message.

4 Type your reply and then click the Send button

5 The reply is moved to your Outbox from where it is sent via your outgoing server

123

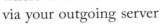

Don't forget

A copy of your reply will be saved in the Sent items folder.

Attachments

Some messages may have files attached, as indicated by the paperclip symbol alongside the Inbox entry.

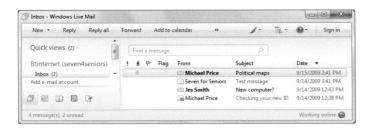

1 Double-click the Inbox entry to open the message

2 Right-click an attachment and select Save all (or Save as, for one file)

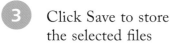

3 Click Save to store the selected files

4 The files are saved in the specified folder, by default the current user's Documents folder

Contacts

You can save email addresses in the Windows Live Mail Contacts folder which acts as an address book.

Don't forget

By default Windows Live Mail puts people you reply to into your Contacts list.

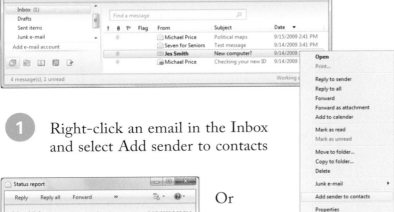

1 Right-click an email in the Inbox and select Add sender to contacts

Or

Open the message and select Add contact, or right click any email address and select Add to contacts

Beware

If the email address is already in the Contacts list, the Add sender options are disabled or removed, and the right-click menu offers to Edit Contact.

125

2 The Add a Contact window opens, with email details

Hot tip

To view and edit your Contacts list, click the Contacts shortcut.

3 Add personal and work information if desired, then click OK to add the details to the Contacts list

Create a Message

1 Open Windows Live Mail, click the Mail shortcut and click the New button to open a message window

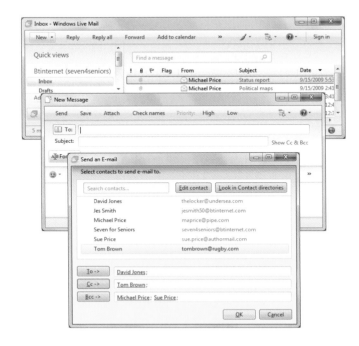

2 Click the To button to open the Contacts, then select names, pressing To, Cc or Bcc after each

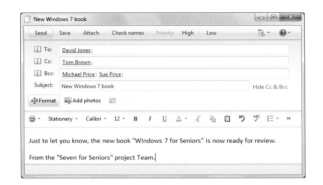

3 Type the Subject for the message, add the message text and end with your signature, then press Send

Junk Mail Protection

Windows Live Mail will check your mail as it is received.

Beware

You'll still need an antivirus program to protect your system (see page 222).

1 Open a message with an executable file, and Windows Live Mail removes access to it, just in case

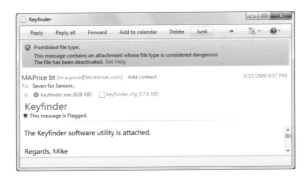

Hot tip

If you are ever unsure of a message that you receive, you can click the Junk button to move it to the Junk folder.

2 Open Junk email to check the messages transferred there and right-click to confirm the required action

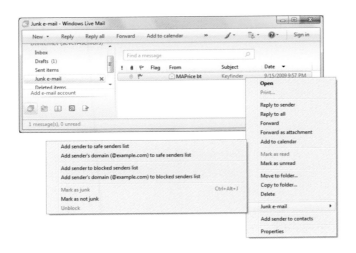

Don't forget

Add the sender (or the sender's domain) to the blocked list or the safe list, as appropriate, and return valid mail to the Inbox.

Calendar

1 Open Windows Live Mail and select Calendar

2 Double-click a time period to define appointments (including recurring appointments) and set reminders

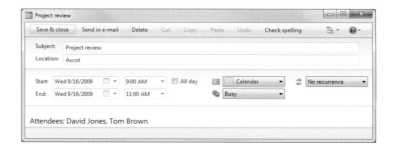

3 Specify whether you are busy or away, and add notes as required, then Click Save & Close to add the item

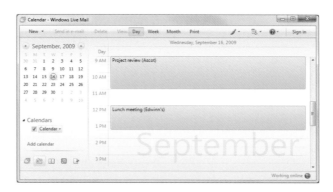

Windows Live Calendar

Windows Live Calendar is an online service which is synchronized with the Windows Live Mail Calendar on your computer. The online calendar can be shared with other Windows Live users, and it can also provide national or regional holiday calendars.

1 Open Windows Live Mail, select Calendar and click the Sign in button

2 Provide your Windows Live ID and password, click Remember my password (optional) and click Sign in

129

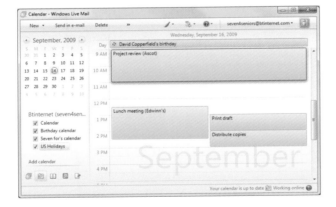

3 The first time you access Windows Live Calendar, the holiday calendar for your country is created

4 A Birthday calendar, based on the personal details stored in your Contacts folder, is also created

5 Clear the box next to any calendar to hide its entries

Webmail

You can access most email accounts using Internet Explorer rather than Windows Live Mail. This means that you can read and send email anywhere that you have Internet access. This could be an Internet cafe, at a hotel or using a wireless hot zone, at an airport for example.

Your ISP will provide details for accessing your account as webmail over the Internet, if this function is supported. Otherwise, you can provide yourself with an account just for webmail. Google, for example, offers free webmail accounts.

Don't forget

In some locations, for example UK and Germany, the email addresses offered will be of the form @googlemail.com and the service is known as Google Mail

1 Go to www.gmail.com and enter your username and password if you already have an account with Google

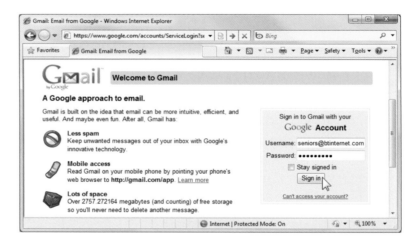

Hot tip

You may already have registered an email address with Google, to use other features. You'll be able to add a Gmail account to this.

2 Otherwise, scroll down and select the option to Create an account with Gmail

...cont'd

3 Provide your name, login name and password, and
follow the prompts to complete your registration

When you've completed your registration and received your
email you can sign in at the www.gmail.com website.

Webmail offers all the functions available in Windows
Live Mail. In addition, it is accessible from anywhere on
the Internet and it allows you to check your mail and
attachments before they are downloaded to your hard disk.

Hot tip

Google will suggest
variations of the
login name that are
available, if your
suggested name is
already in use.

131

Don't forget

Google does permit
you to access your
webmail account using
POP3 email software
such as Windows Live
Mail, so you could
restrict webmail access
to the times when you
are away from your
normal system.

Instant Messaging

When you have registered your Windows Live ID, you can use it to sign in to Windows Live Messenger, another of the Windows Live Essentials (see page 37). This supports Instant Messaging, which allows you to send and receive instant messages. To sign in:

 **1** Windows Live Messenger usually appears during Windows startup

132

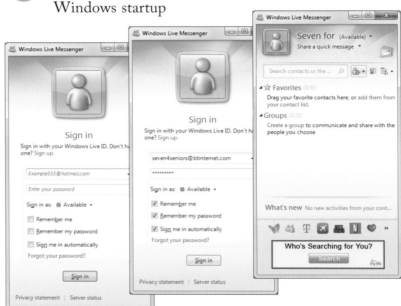

2 Enter Windows Live ID and password, then click Sign in

3 Click Add a contact or group and then select Add a contact

 4 Add your Contact's Instant Messaging details

5   Add a message if desired, then click Send Invitation, as an Instant message and as an email

Hot tip

If your contact is not already a member of Windows Live Messenger, the email will prompt the person to join.

6   Your contact must accept the invitation, by email or through instant messaging, before being added

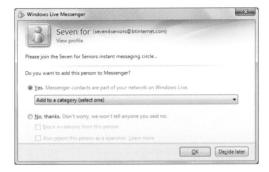

Don't forget

If there are numerous contacts, organize them into associated groups, or select the more significant ones as Favorites.

7   Windows Live Messenger will show the contacts that have been added to your circle, and will display their current status

If you receive invitations from people you don't know, you can say No to the requests. There will be no feedback to the originator. If appropriate, you can choose to block future invites from those people or report them as spammers.

Newsgroups

1 Open Windows Live Mail, Newsgroups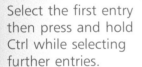
and select View Newsgroups

2 Specify a topic to list relevant newsgroups, choose
those of interest and select Subscribe and then OK

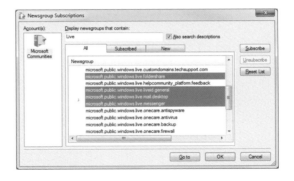

3 Select the news server from the Folders list and click
a newsgroup to review the message exchanges

8 Internet

The addition of tabbed browsing helps you navigate through the Web without losing track of useful web pages. The Favorites Center includes history and feeds as well as favorites. You can specify your preferred search engines, use the page zoom feature to focus on detailed contents, and track web page changes.

Connect to the Internet

To set up an Internet account directly from your computer:

1 Click the Start button, select Control Panel, then select Connect to the Internet (in the Network and Internet category)

2 The Connect to the Internet wizard starts up and asks the type of connection, e.g. Broadband or Dialup

3 Select the type, provide details, e.g. phone number (dialup only), account name and password, click Connect to complete the connection definition

You can also make use of an existing Internet connection provided by a networked computer or via a Broadband modem and network router or wireless hub. See page 204 for more information about networks.

Use an Existing Connection

1 Select Control Panel and click the entry View network status and tasks.
Your computer will initially show as disconnected

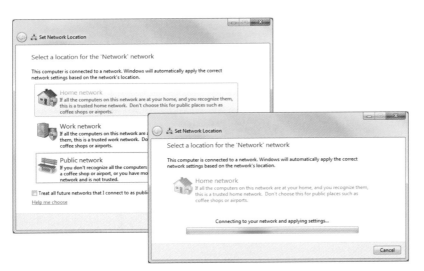

Don't forget

Windows 7 will automatically detect network and Internet connections, during installation or the first time you enable your network adapter.

2 Connect your adapter to the network and Windows 7 will ask you to specify the type of network

137

Hot tip

You will be given the opportunity to create a HomeGroup (see page 206), or click Cancel and create the HomeGroup later.

3 Network and Sharing Center shows the connections

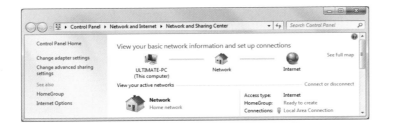

Browse the Web

Windows 7 provides Internet Explorer v8.0 as the default
Web browser.

Don't forget

Right-click the Internet
Explorer entry and
select Pin to Start
menu, to place an
entry at the top of the
Start menu.

1 Click the Internet
Explorer shortcut
on the Taskbar, or select Start, All
Programs, and click Internet Explorer

Network and Internet
Connect to the Internet
View network status and tasks
Choose homegroup and sharing options

Internet Explorer

2 The first time you open Internet Explorer, it asks you
to confirm the settings you require

Don't forget

Suggested Sites is an
online service designed
to suggest other
websites you might be
interested in, based on
the websites you visit
most often.

Set Up Windows Internet Explorer 8

Welcome to Internet Explorer 8

Internet Explorer 8 helps you use the Internet even faster than before.

New features like search suggestions retrieve information as you type,
and Accelerators let you preview online services just by pointing your
mouse at them.

Learn about these new features and how to manage their settings

Next   Ask me later

Set Up Windows Internet Explorer 8

Turn on Suggested Sites

Do you want to discover websites you might like based on websites
you've visited?

☑ Yes, turn on Suggested Sites

○ No, don't turn on

Suggested Sites is an online service
website suggestions. You can turn

Read the Internet Explorer Privacy Statement

Set Up Windows Internet Explorer 8

Choose your settings

Before you get started, do you want to:

☑ Use express settings
Search provider: Bing
Search Updates: Download provider updates
Accelerators: Blog with Windows Live, Map with Bing, E-mail with Windows Live,
Translate with Bing
Compatibility View: Use updates

○ Choose custom settings
Review and modify each setting individually.

Read the Internet Explorer Privacy Statement online   Back   Finish   Cancel

3 Postpone until later, or decide the settings for
Suggested Sites, Search Provider, Accelerators, etc

4 Internet Explorer displays your Home page (the default startup website), in this case www.nga.gov

5 Move the mouse pointer over the window and where it changes to the hand symbol there's a hyperlink that you can click to view another web page

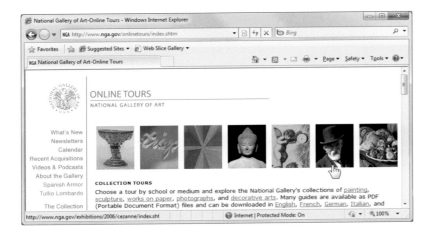

6 Images and graphics as well as text can have hyperlinks associated with them

Navigating

The Back and Forward buttons allow you to switch between pages.

1 Click Back to return to the previous web page

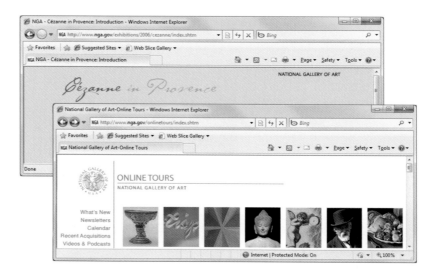

Hyperlinks can be associated with images, and tool tips may be used to explain the purpose of the link.

2 Click and drag the scroll bar or click the scroll bar buttons to view other parts of the web page

Selecting Open Link will display the page in the same window, just as when you click a hyperlink. Pressing Ctrl when you click is the same as selecting Open in New Tab.

3 Right-click the hyperlink and select Open in New Tab to display the specified web page in the same window but on a separate tab (see next page)

4 Open in New Window would display the page in a new Internet Explorer window

Tabbed Browsing

When you select Show Link on New Tab, the new tab is added but the original tab remains displayed.

Don't forget

With Ctrl+Click, the tab opens in the background. If, however, you press Ctrl+Shift+Click, the new tab opens in the foreground.

1 Select the new tab to view the web page it contains

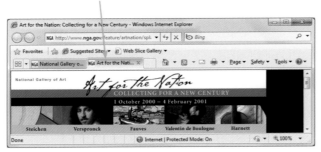

2 Select the first tab, then choose other hyperlinks and open them in new tabs, or click the New Tab button at the end of the tab bar to open a blank tab

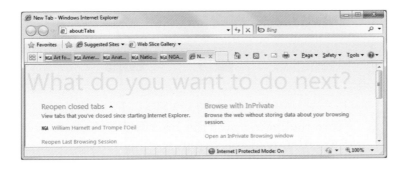

Hot tip

The New Tab button gives you a blank tab where you can enter a URL on the address bar, or redisplay the previously viewed web pages.

3 From here you can view tabs closed during the current browsing session, or reopen the last session

Quick Tabs

When you have a number of tabs open, their titles become truncated and some tabs may be hidden. To help you select the tab you want, the Tab row is extended to show the Quick Tabs button, plus the Scroll buttons when required.

1 Click the Scroll buttons to reveal the hidden tabs

2 Click the arrow next to the Quick Tabs button to select a tab by the web page title

3 Click the Quick Tabs button to display thumbnails of all the open web pages and click one to select it

4 Move the mouse over the Internet Explorer icon on the taskbar to display icons for the tabs and windows

Close Tabs

1 To close the current tab, click the X on the tab (or press Ctrl+W or press Alt+F4)

2 To close all the tabs except the current tab, press Ctrl+Alt+F4

3 To close the Internet Explorer session, click the X on the window title bar, or click the icon on the left and select Close or press Alt+F4

4 If there's more than one tab open, you are prompted to select Close all tabs or Current tab

If you close all tabs Internet Explorer closes. The next time you start Internet Explorer, you can reopen all those tabs.

1 Open a new tab (see page 141) and select Reopen last browsing session

(see page 141)

Hot tip

From the Quick Tabs view, click the [X] on any thumbnail to close that web page.
If you have a wheel mouse, click a tab on the tab row with the wheel to close that tab.

Hot tip

Click the [X] button to cancel, if you decide you do not want to close any of the tabs at this time.

Don't forget

This is useful for continuing work in progress, but if you will need the same set of web pages at a later date, save them as a group favorite.

Add to Favorites

When you visit a web page that you'll want to view again in future, you can save it as a Favorite.

1 With the web page displayed, click the Favorites button and then click Add to Favorites

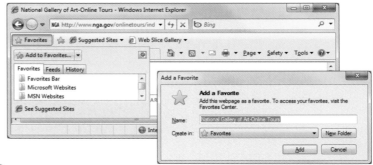

2 Click Add to put the named entry in the main folder

3 To save the set of open tabs as a group, you'd click the down-arrow and select Add Current Tabs to Favorites

4 Provide a Folder Name for the group of tabs and click Add

Favorites Center

To make use of the entries saved in your Favorites list:

1 Click the Favorites button, then select the whole tab group, a web page from within the group, or a web page saved individually

Search for Websites

You can type website addresses on the address bar but the easiest way to locate a website is to use the Search bar.

1 Type key words into the search box, for example Saks 5th Avenue, and press Enter

2 Choose a suitable match and click the link in the header to go to the website

3 Follow hyperlinks in the web page to open other pages on the same tab or in new tabs (see page 141)

(see page 141)

Don't forget

As you type, the search engine suggests search strings that might be appropriate. If the required text appears, just click it.

Beware

The first few results are sponsored sites and paid adverts, so look beyond these for the websites that best match the search text.

Alternative Search Providers

By default, Internet Explorer uses Microsoft's Bing Search but you can choose other providers.

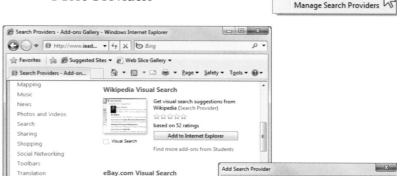

1 Click the arrow next to the Search box and select Find More Providers

2 Locate a provider, e.g. Wikipedia, click Add to Internet Explorer then Add

3 Choose another search provider, e.g. Google, click Make this my default search provider, and click Add

4 The default provider will be updated

5 To use an alternative provider, click the Search box arrow and select the provider, which will stay as the active provider for the remainder of the session

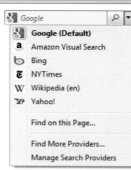

Page Zoom

You may find some web pages difficult to read, especially if you have your monitor set for high resolution. The Page Zoom feature provides an effective solution to this problem.

1 Click the arrow next to Zoom on the status bar

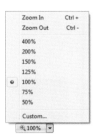

147

2 Choose the zoom level, e.g. 200%

3 Click Zoom to revert to the 100% zoom level

4 Click the Zoom button repeatedly to cycle through the levels 125%, 150% and 100%

5 Select Custom on the Zoom menu, to specify an exact zoom factor, between 10% and 1000%

Print Web Page

1 Open Internet Explorer, navigate to the web page and make sure that it is displayed on the active tab

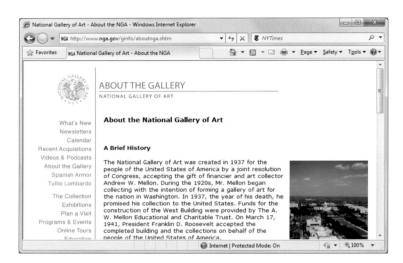

148

2 Click the down-arrow next to the Print button and select the Print Preview option

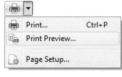

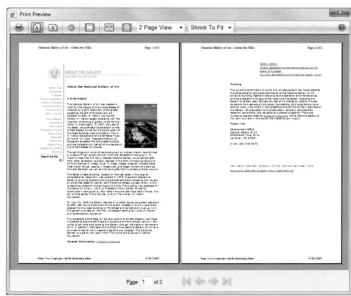

If Shrink To Fit makes the web page too small to read comfortably, you can try changing the page orientation to increase the width available for printing. For example:

The Shrink to Fit value for Portrait was 67%, but for Landscape it becomes 100%.

1 Select the Landscape button in Print Preview, and make sure that Shrink To Fit is being applied

2 To see more pages at once, click the Page View box and select the appropriate number of pages, e.g. 3

Select a scale factor up to 200% (or a custom value up to 999%) for a larger print copy.

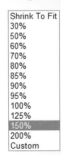

3 To print part of the page, highlight the area, choose Print Preview, then select As selected on screen

4 Click the Printer button to complete the operation

149

RSS Feeds

An RSS feed (also known as a web feed) is a means of collating updates to web pages so you can be made aware of changes without having to revisit the website. Internet Explorer tells you whenever there's a feed available.

1 If there are no feeds available, the Feeds button on the toolbar will be grayed

2 When you switch to a web page that has a feed, the Feeds button changes color and a sound plays

3 Click Feeds to view the reports and to subscribe

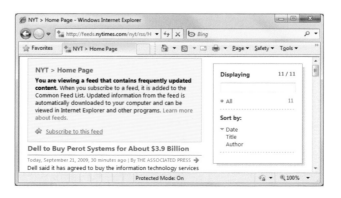

Hot tip

In the original standard, the abbreviation RSS stood for RDF (Resource Description Framework) Site Summary. Later it became Rich Site Summary but the latest interpretation is Really Simple Syndication.

Don't forget

Click the down arrow to see how many feeds there are on the page (e.g. there are two for CNN.com).

Don't forget

You can review the contents and then click Subscribe to this feed, if you are interested in more updates.

4 Change the name for the feed if desired, then click Subscribe

5 Your subscription will be confirmed

Hot tip

Specify a folder name, to help organize groups of feeds.

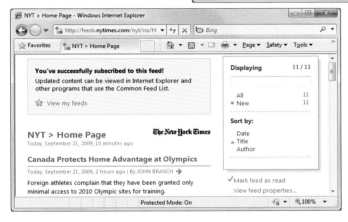

Don't forget

You can sort the feed into Date, Title or Author. Click View feed properties... to turn on sound signal or specify retention period, etc.

6 To view your subscribed feeds, click the Favorites Center button and then click Feeds

Don't forget

Windows Live Mail will also manage RSS Feeds. Click the Feeds shortcut to display available messages.

7 Subscriptions with new content are highlighted

8 Click any entry to review its contents

History

Don't forget

Internet Explorer keeps track of the websites that you have visited in the last 20 days.

Don't forget

To close the Favorites Center when you've finished with history, click the [X] button at the top right.

1 Click the Favorites Center button and select History

2 Click the green arrow to pin the Favorites Center to keep it displayed until closed

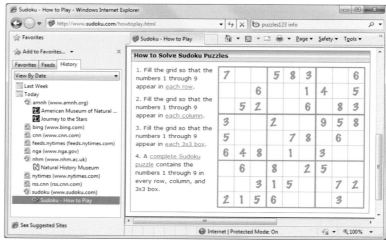

3 Click a period, e.g. Today, click a website header to list the web pages visited, then select a web page

4 To clear the history, click the Safety button and select Delete Browsing History

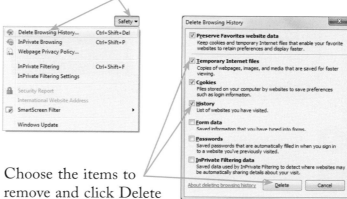

5 Choose the items to remove and click Delete

9 Windows Applications

Windows includes some surprisingly useful applications for calculating, text editing, word processing and picture editing, but you need external programs to handle files unknown to the default setup.

Applications

Windows provides the operating environment for a variety of applications. In many cases, these are supplied as separate programs or suite of programs. However, some of the desired functions may be in the form of small but potentially very useful programs included with Windows or Windows Live Essentials (see page 37). The main application areas and the related Windows programs are:

- Text processing   Notepad
- Word processing   WordPad
- Electronic Mail   [see chapter 7]
- Drawing   Paint
- Spreadsheet   Calculator only
- Database   [no program]
- Multimedia   [see chapter 12]

Don't forget

These applications take advantage of Windows 7 features such as Aero and Flip 3D, but may use older Windows features such as menu bars.

154

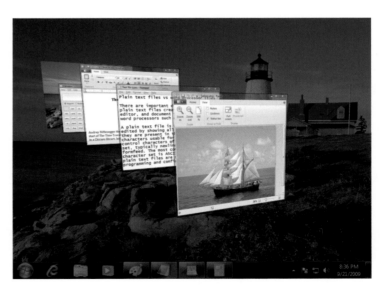

For requirements that are not supported by the programs in Windows, you'll need to install separate programs or a suite of programs such as Adobe Acrobat or Microsoft Office. Even if you don't have these you may need readers and viewers, free programs that allow you to view the files created by those separate applications.

Don't forget

We show you where you can find these applications and what's involved with downloading and installing them.

Calculator

While no substitute for a spreadsheet application, Windows Calculator provides quite powerful computational facilities.

1. Select Start, All Programs, Accessories, Calculator

2. Type or click to enter the first number, the operation symbol and the next number

3. Enter any additional operators and numbers and press = to finish

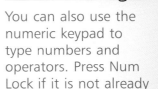

You click the calculator buttons or press the equivalent keyboard keys, to perform Add, Subtract, Multiply, Divide, Square Root, Percent and Inverse operations. You can also store and recall numbers from memory, and the History capability keeps track of stages in the calculations.

Scientific, Programmer and Statistics views are also provided:

1. Open Calculator, select View and choose, for example Scientific

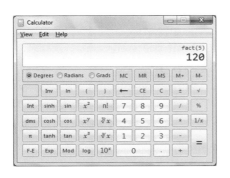

The Scientific calculator includes a variety of functions and inverse functions, including logarithms and factorials.

Windows Calculator also supports unit conversions, date calculations and some basic worksheet functions for mortgage, vehicle lease and fuel economy calculations.

155

Don't forget

You can also use the numeric keypad to type numbers and operators. Press Num Lock if it is not already turned on.

Don't forget

The programmer view supports hexadecimal, decimal, octal and binary numbers.

Hot tip

Calculator clears the display when you switch views. Use the memory button to transfer a number between two modes.

Notepad

Notepad is a text editor that you can use to create, view or modify text (.txt) files. It provides only very basic formatting, and handles text a line at a time.

1 Select Start, All Programs, Accessories, Notepad and type some text, pressing Enter to start a new line

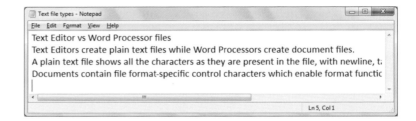

2 Select File, Save As and type the required file name (with file type .txt) then click Save

3 To show the whole of the long text lines in the window, select Format and click Word Wrap

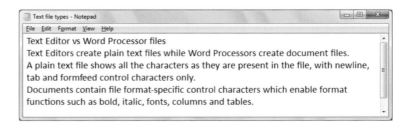

4 When you print the file, it will wrap according to the paper width, regardless of the word-wrap setting

WordPad

WordPad also offers text-editing, but adds tools and facilities for complex formatting of individual pieces of text.

1 Select Start, All Programs, Accessories, WordPad and enter text, pressing Enter to start a new paragraph

2 Use the formatting bar to change the font, size, style and color for selected (highlighted) text

3 Click the Save button on the Quick Access Toolbar (or click the WordPad button and select File, Save, or press Ctrl+S)

Insert Pictures

WordPad also allows you to include pictures in documents.

1 Position the typing cursor, and click the Picture button in the Insert group on the Home tab

2 Locate and select the picture file then click Open

3 A copy of the image is added to the document, and displayed at the cursor location

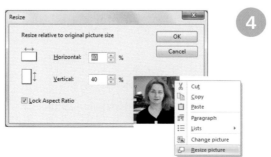

4 Right-click the picture and select Resize picture, and choose the scale required

Paint

Paint is a digital sketchpad that can be used to draw, color and edit pictures. These can be images that you create from scratch, or you can modify existing pictures, such as digital photographs or a web page graphics. For example:

1 Select Start, All Programs, Accessories, Paint to open with a blank canvas

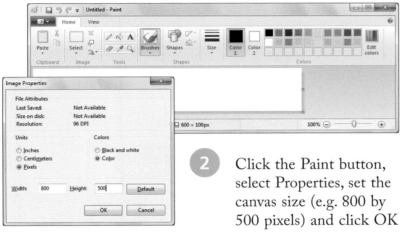

Hot tip

Although it is a simple image editor, Paint can be used to create very complex images, a pixel at a time if required.

2 Click the Paint button, select Properties, set the canvas size (e.g. 800 by 500 pixels) and click OK

3 Select the arrow below Paste, select Paste From, locate a picture to add to the canvas and click Open

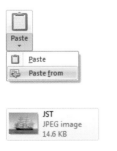

4 Drag the image to position it

Don't forget

If the pasted image is larger than the canvas, the canvas will automatically be extended to hold the picture.

...cont'd

5 Select the Rounded Rectangle tool then click and drag to draw a frame around the picture

Hot tip

Draw a second frame and use the Fill tool to color the space between the frames.

6 Use the Text tool to draw a text box and add information such as a description of the contents

7 To make changes, select the Home tab, Magnifier or the View tab, Zoom in

8 When you've finished making changes, select File, Save, type the file name and click Save

Don't forget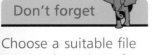

Choose a suitable file type such as .jpeg for pictures, or .gif for sketches. Paint also supports .bmp, .tif and .png file formats.

Unknown File Types

Windows and its applications cannot help when you receive attachments or download files of unknown file types.

1 If there are unknown file types in your Documents folder, the extensions (normally hidden) are displayed

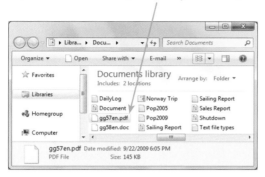

Don't forget

Windows supports a set of file types (as indicated by the file extension). If you have additional programs installed, there may be further known file extensions on your system.

2 Double-click an unknown file type, e.g. gg57en.pdf, and you are warned Windows cannot open this file

Beware

When the Web service is unable to find the type, it will suggest www.filext.com, a website with a more comprehensive list.

3 Click OK to use the Web service to display details of the file type and suggested programs to open it

Hot tip

See page 162 for the information provided for .pdf files, and page 164 for .doc files.

Portable Document Format

The Web service provides information for .pdf files.

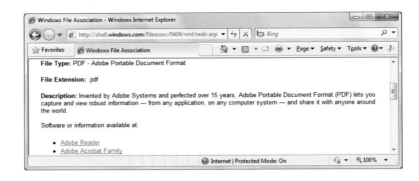

① To view the contents of .pdf documents, click Adobe Reader and select your operating system version

② Click Continue, clear box if you don't want the Free Google Toolbar, then select Download now to begin the download and installation

3 Follow the prompts to download, install and configure the Adobe Reader application

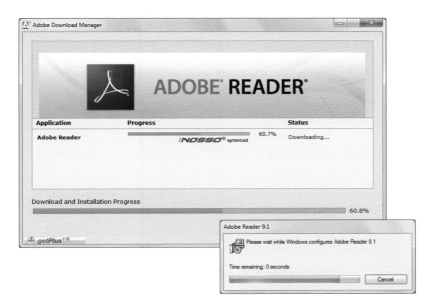

4 When this completes, Windows will now recognize the .pdf file type

5 You will now be able to open and read your .pdf files

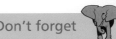

Don't forget

An entry for Adobe Reader will be added to the Start menu under All Programs, and it will also appear highlighted as a newly installed program

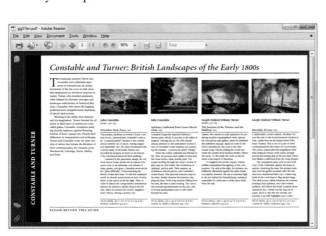

Word Document Files

Don't forget

Programs from both Microsoft and Corel, for creating and modifying .doc files, are suggested.

The Web service also provides suggestions for .doc files, not recognized by Windows without additional software.

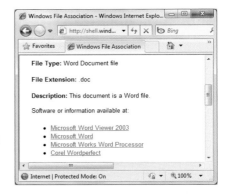

1 To be able to view the contents of .doc documents, select Word Viewer 2003

Hot tip

Microsoft also provides viewers for other Office applications, including Access, Excel, PowerPoint and Visio.

2 Click Download to transfer the file

3 Select Save to store the installation file on your hard disk

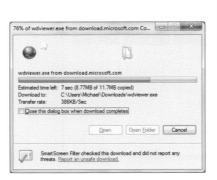

4 Double-click the downloaded file to install Word Viewer

5 Follow the Setup program prompts to complete the installation and configuration of Word Viewer 2003

Don't forget

An entry for Microsoft Office Word Viewer 2003 will be added to the Start menu under All Programs.

6 You will now be able to open and read .doc files

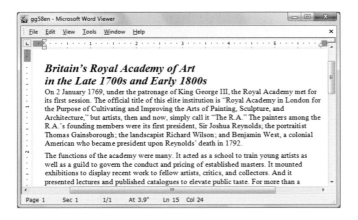

The .doc extension for document files will now be hidden.

Beware

Word Viewer will also become the default program for the .rtf (Rich Text Format) files previously handled by WordPad.

Change Default Program

To restore WordPad as the default program for .rtf files:

1 Right-click any .rtf file and select Open With

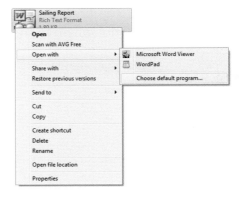

2 Select WordPad, select Always use the selected program to open this kind of file, and click OK

3 The .rtf files now have WordPad as the default

10 Windows Games

Windows provides
an endless source of
entertainment, with a
variety of games to both
challenge and teach,
and you can play alone
or against human or
computer opponents, at
home or online using your
Internet connection.

Games Explorer

The Games Explorer identifies the games supplied with Windows 7 or installed on your computer and provides access to them via the Games folder.

1 Click the Start button and select Games

2 The games folder opens, showing six games for Starter or Home Basic editions

3 With the other editions, Premium games are included, giving you a total of eleven games

4 There are three games that are Internet based, so you can play online against human opponents

Turn On Games

On your particular system, you may find some or all of the games missing when you open the Games folder.

The missing games will have been turned off. To add or remove games in the Games folder:

1 Select Start, Control Panel and then click Programs

2 Select Turn Windows features on and off

3 Click the box next to Games to turn on all the items

or

4 Click the [+] to expand the list, select individual games and then click OK

5 Windows makes the requested changes to the features

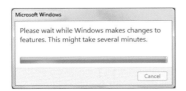

Don't forget

Business oriented editions such as Enterprise include games, but by default they are not enabled.

169

Hot tip

This option controls the use of many Windows features including Gadgets, Internet Explorer, DVD Maker, Media Center, Media Player and XPS Viewer. Note that turning off will not uninstall the feature.

Exploring Games

The first time you open the Games folder, you are asked if you want to use the recommended settings.

If you select this option, Windows will automatically:

- Notify you of games news or software updates

- Download art and information about the games

- Show when you last played a particular game

1 Open the Games folder and click on a specific game

2 The Details pane shows publisher and developer

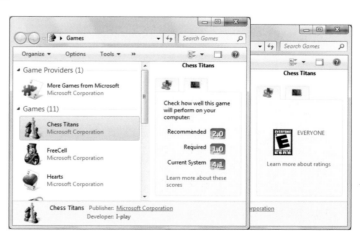

3 The Preview pane shows the hardware requirements needs or the game rating

4 Windows 7 games are all rated for Everyone

Don't forget

The games use the ESRB (Entertainment Software Rating Board) ratings or the regional equivalent, for example PEGI (Pan European Game Information) in Europe.

Chess Titans

1 Double-click Chess Titans in the Games folder to begin a game (or continue the last game)

Hot tip

You can play against the computer or at home against another person (who would share your mouse to make moves).

2 Click a piece to see the legal moves (these are colored blue, or red where you can take a piece)

3 Click Game to choose a new opponent, change appearance or resign a game

Game	
New game against computer	F2
New game against human	F3
Undo	Ctrl+Z
Statistics	F4
Options	F5
Change Appearance	F7
Resign	
Exit	

Don't forget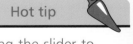

Chess Titans keeps track of all the games you play and shows your results when you select statistics.

4 Click Options to change graphics quality and other settings

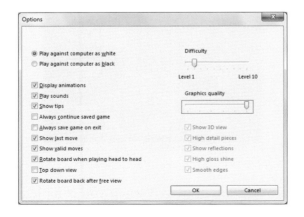

Hot tip

Drag the slider to the left to turn off graphics quality options progressively.

Mahjong Titans

It is simple to get started with this game and it needs only one player. However, it takes a surprising amount of strategy and planning to achieve high scores.

1 Double-click Mahjong Titans in the Games folder

2 Select one of the six layouts, e.g. Dragon

3 Click matching pairs of free tiles to remove them

4 If you (or your grandchild) get stuck, select Game, Hint and two matching tiles will flash

5 Select Change Appearance to choose an alternative tile set

6 Fireworks are displayed when you complete a game

Minesweeper

1 Double-click Minesweeper in the Games folder

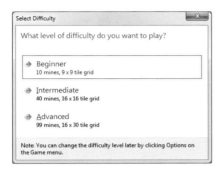 

Hot tip

The first time you play, you'll be asked to select the level of difficulty.

Click a square on the playing field. If a number appears on a square, it indicates how many total mines are in the eight squares that surround the numbered square.

2 If you uncover a mine, all the mines explode and you've lost the game

Don't forget

You use the number to help deduce whether a square is safe to uncover. Right-click a suspect square to add a flag, or double right-click to add a ? mark.

173

3 Click Play again for a new game, or Restart this game to try it again, or Exit to finish playing

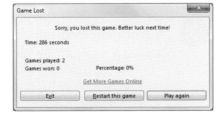

Don't forget

Choose flowers as an alternative to mines, but they'll still explode if you click on them.

4 Click Game to start a new game, view the statistics, adjust the options or change the appearance

Purble Place

This set of games is educational and entertaining, and helps to teach colors, shapes and pattern recognition and to encourage deduction. There are three games included: Purble Pairs, Comfy Cakes and Purble Shop

1 Open Purble Place, and select one of the games, for example the middle entry Comfy Cakes

2 Select Game, Options (or press F5) to set the difficulty level

3 Select matching options for shape, fill and covering, working against the clock

FreeCell

FreeCell is a variant of solitaire. To win, you must stack the four suits in ascending order (ace to king). You draw cards from seven columns of cards that you build in descending order, alternating red and black. Free cells are used to hold cards temporarily while you rearrange sequences.

Don't forget

There are one million different games in FreeCell, all of which are solvable except for games numbered 11982, 146692, 186216, 455889, 495505, 512118, 517776 and 781948.

1 Double-click FreeCell to deal out a random game (or continue with a previously saved game)

2 Click Game then Select Game (or press F3) and enter a game number between 1 and 1000000

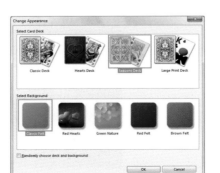

Beware

Selecting a new game number will count as a loss in your statistics, if the current game has already been started.

3 Click Game then Change Appearance to select a new card deck style or play area background

Other Card Games

Hearts

You play in rounds against three computer opponents. The aim is to avoid taking the hearts and the queen of spades.

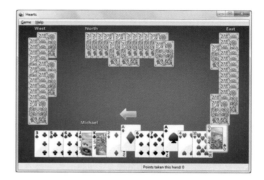

Solitaire

Solitaire is based on the traditional Klondike solitaire.

Don't forget

You must build four stacks of cards, by suit and in ascending order (ace to king). To build these stacks, you draw from seven columns of cards that you build in descending order, alternating red and black.

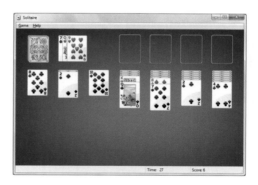

Spider Solitaire

Spider Solitaire uses two decks (104 cards).

Don't forget

The objective is to line up cards in runs (king to ace) to remove all the cards from the ten stacks at the top of the window in the fewest moves.

Internet Games

Premium editions of Windows 7 include several multiplayer games. These allow you to play online against human or computer opponents. You need to be connected to the Internet to play these games.

Internet Backgammon
This is a two-person board game where you aim to be the first to move all your pieces around and off the board. Roll the two dice to decide how far you move on your turn.

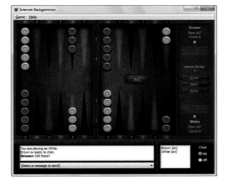

Internet Checkers
This is an online version of one of the oldest and most popular games in the world. You must capture all your opponent's checkers or block all your opponent's legal moves.

Internet Spades
This is a fast-paced card game that demands teamwork and strategy. The Spades suit is always Trumps. You and your partner guess how many tricks you will win. You are awarded points for making your contract (or penalized for failing).

More Internet Games

If you enjoy playing games on the computer but want a different selection:

1 Open the Games folder and choose one of the Games providers to see what's offered

2 Click More Games to visit MSN Games Zone and play a suggested game, or click View more games

11 Music and Audio

Create recordings, play audio CDs and convert tracks to computer files. Build and manage a music and sound library.

Sound Card and Speakers

Hot tip

You can also open System Properties by selecting View computer details in Welcome Center.

The sound card in your computer processes the information from programs such as Windows Media Player and sends audio signals to your computer's speakers. To identify your card:

1 Press Windows Logo+Pause keys to open System Properties, and click Device Manager

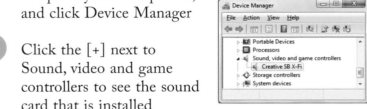

2 Click the [+] next to Sound, video and game controllers to see the sound card that is installed

Don't forget

You may have sound features incorporated into the main system board, rather than on a separate adapter.

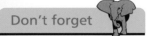

3 To configure your sound setup, open Control Panel and select Hardware and Sound, and then Sound

Hardware and Sound
View devices and printers
Add a device

Sound
Adjust system volume
Change system sounds
Manage audio devices

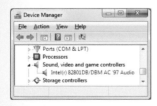

4 Click the Playback tab, select the entry for speakers and click Configure

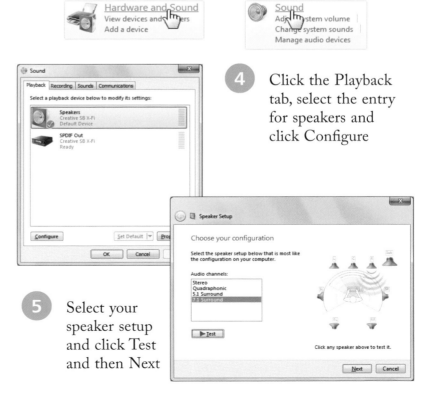

5 Select your speaker setup and click Test and then Next

6 Specify which speakers are present in your setup

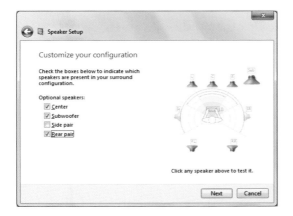

7 Click Finish to complete the configuration

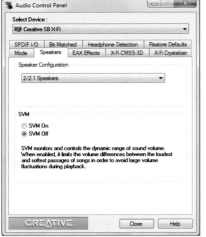

8 If you have a separate adapter card, it may be supplied with its own audio application program to help you set up, configure and test the device features

Recording

Don't forget

Other sources could include Line-In (audio device), Digital-In (CD or DVD drive) or What U Hear (anything that is being played through the sound card, including web broadcasts for example).

With a sound card on your system, you can make voice recordings from a microphone or other audio sources. To set up your microphone:

1 Open the Sound option from the Control Panel (see page 90) and click the Recording tab

2 Select the Microphone entry and click Configure

Don't forget

A headset microphone is the best choice if you are considering use of voice control.

3 Select Set up microphone and select the type in use

4 Read the sample text and follow the prompts to set up the microphone for best recordings

If the microphone recording level is too low:

5 Click the Microphone Properties button on the Sound, Recording tab

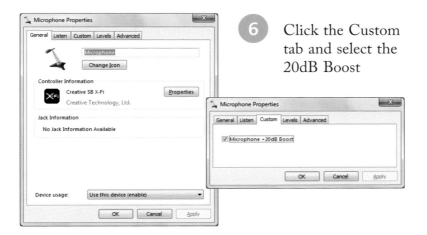

6 Click the Custom tab and select the 20dB Boost

Make a Recording

Programs (1)
🎙 Sound Recorder

1 Click the Start button, search for Recorder and select the program Sound Recorder

2 Click Start Recording button and say your message

3 Click Stop Recording and provide a name for the audio file that will be created

Hot tip

Alternatively select Start, All Programs, Accessories and then click Sound Recorder.

183

Don't forget

The file is created as type Windows Media Audio (.wma).

Windows Media Player

To play the recorded sound file:

1 Open the folder containing the file, and double-click the file icon to start Windows Media Player

2 The first time, you must choose the settings required

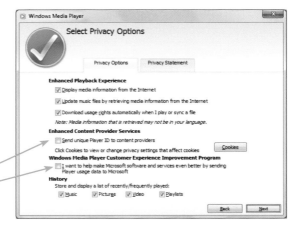

Don't forget

Leave the boxes clear if you'd prefer not to send information about your playing experiences.

3 Make any changes you wish, then click Next

4 Confirm Windows Media Player as your default music and video player and click Finish

The recorded item plays in Windows Media Player. It is treated as if it is a music track, and it quotes any artist and album details that you provided when you created the file.

1 Move the mouse pointer over the Now Playing windows to display the progress bar and play tools

2 Right-click the Now Playing window area to display the options and select Enhancements

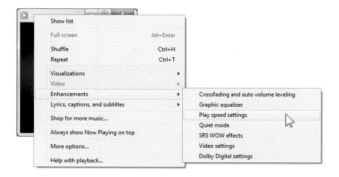

Don't forget

Selecting any of these will give the Show Enhancements arrows. Click these arrows to scroll back and forth through the enhancements.

3 Choose the enhancements Play Speed Settings

4 Move the Play Speed slider, or click the Slow, Normal or Fast link to select the playback speed

Hot tip

You can speed up a voice recording to get an overview or slow it down to help with note taking. The sound maintains correct pitch when the playback speed changes.

Play Audio CD

1 Insert an audio CD and close the drive

2 Windows recognizes the type of disc and asks you what to do (if the default action hasn't already been defined)

3 Click Play audio CD using Windows Media Player and the CD will play

4 Right-click Now Playing and select Show list. The first time you play a CD, the tracks are unidentified

5 If you are connected to the Internet, the player will identify the specific disc and download track details

Copy Tracks

1 Right-click Now Playing, select More Options, then click the Rip Music tab

2 For Format, choose the type of audio file (e.g. MP3)

3 Choose the Audio Quality (e.g. using bit rate 192 Kbps)

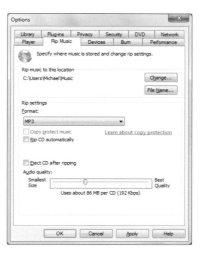

4 Start playing the CD, and click the Rip CD button

5 Each track in turn is copied, converted and saved

Hot tip

Tracks will be saved by default in your Music folder. Select More Options to change the location.

Beware

The higher the bit rate, the better the quality but the larger the file. As an estimate, a full audio disc copied at:

Bit rate	Needs
128 Kbps	57 MB
192	86
256	115
320	144

Don't forget

You can play the CD while tracks are being independently copied (at a multiple of the standard play speed – the whole CD may be completed before the first track finishes playing).

Media Library

The converted tracks will be saved in the Artist/Album subfolder of the specified location, e.g. the Music folder.

To play the tracks from the hard disk:

1 Start the Windows Media Player and click the Library button to switch to the Library view

2 Choose how to display the contents of the Music library, e.g. by Album or Artist

3 Double-click an artist to display the albums. Double-click an album to start it playing

12 Pictures and Videos

Import digital images from your camera or from media cards. Windows Live Photo Gallery helps you organize your collections and create movies or DVDs. For a complete media system, use Windows Media Center.

Digital Pictures

There are a number of ways you can obtain digital pictures:

- Internet (e.g. art and photography websites)
- Scanner (copies of documents, photographs or slides)
- Digital Camera (photographs and movies)
- Email attachments and faxes

Website pictures will usually be stored as JPEG (.jpg) files, which are compressed to minimize the file size. This preserves the full color range but there is some loss of quality. Some images such as graphic symbols and buttons will use the GIF (.gif) format, which restricts color to 256 shades to minimize the file size. To copy a digital image from a website such as www.wikipedia.org:

1. Right-click the image and select Save Picture As

2. Type a suitable file name and click Save

3 Select Start, Pictures and select the appropriate subfolder to list and view the saved images

Hot tip

You can also view your downloaded pictures in the Windows Live Photo Gallery (see page 194).

Websites may sometimes offer you the option to download higher quality images. For example, en.wikipedia.org/wiki/Salisbury_Cathedral_from_the_Bishop%27s_Grounds:

1 This entry shows Constable's Salisbury Cathedral from the Bishop's Grounds at a size of 325 x 253

2 Click the image and you'll see a preview 770 x 579, with a link to a full resolution image 3176 x 2472

Beware

Images downloaded from websites are usually copyrighted and provided for personal use only.

Import from Camera

To transfer pictures from your camera to your computer:

1 Connect the camera to a USB port on your computer, and turn on the camera

2 On the camera, choose to connect to the PC

3 The first time you connect, the necessary device driver will be installed

4 Choose to Import pictures using Windows Live Photo Gallery

5 Click Import all new items now and enter folder name

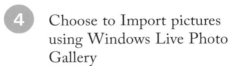

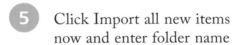

6 The items are copied to the Pictures library

Media Card Readers

If your camera uses a removable memory card such as Secure Digital or Compact Flash, you may be able to read the card directly, without having to attach the camera.

1 Insert the memory card into the appropriate reader slot to display the AutoPlay dialog

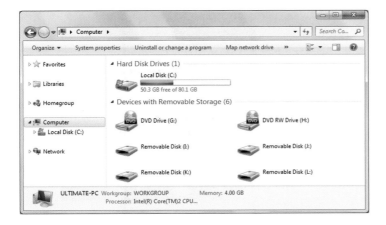

2 Import pictures using Windows Live Photo Gallery

3 If there are pictures from several dates, choose Review, organize and group items to import

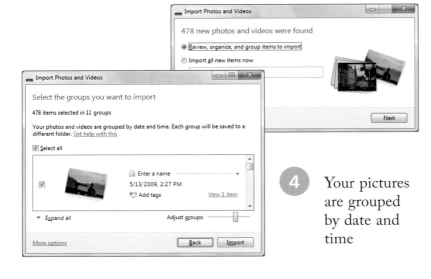

4 Your pictures are grouped by date and time

Hot tip

The media card reader can handle a variety of memory cards. In this example there are four slots, each with a different drive letter.

193

Don't forget

Right-click the Safely Remove Hardware icon and select the entry for your camera or media card, before removing the device.

Windows Live Photo Gallery

Whenever you import pictures, the Photo Gallery will open.

1 Click the triangle next to a category heading such as Tags or Date Taken to expand the list of values

2 Choose, for example, the Flowers tag to see all associated pictures or videos

Add Tags

1 Display the pictures you want to tag (e.g. by date taken or by folder) and select one or more images

Don't forget

You can specify tags when you import the pictures from your camera or media card.

2 Drag the selection over a descriptive tag to apply it to the pictures. To see the details, click the Info button

Hot tip

You can click Add descriptive tags on the Info panel to create a new tag or choose an existing tag to apply to the selected pictures.

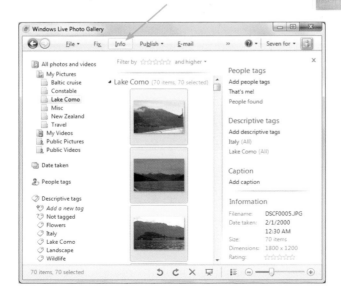

Fix Pictures

1 Double-click any picture to enlarge it

2 Click left and right arrows to scroll through the pictures, and click Fix button to make adjustments

3 Click Auto Adjust to enhance the appearance, or select the individual tools to make custom changes

196

Burn to Disc

If you have a CD or DVD writer on your computer, you can make copies of your pictures, as data files or as a slide show.

1 Select the pictures that you want to save then click the Make button and choose the type of copy

2 To make a backup of your files, select Burn a data CD and insert a writable disc when prompted

3 Edit the title (the current date) if required then choose With a CD/DVD player for the most flexible format

4 Delete any files that are not required then click Burn to disc to complete the transfer

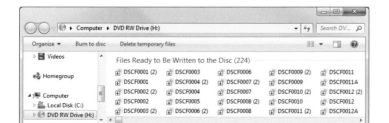

Don't forget

Using the Mastered format creates a CD or DVD that can be read by previous versions of Windows and by other devices such as CD and DVD players.

Hot tip

The files are written to the root folder of the CD, without folder names. Duplicate file names are amended, for example 001.jpg, and 001.jpg (2).

Video DVD

To create a slide show, perhaps with music or commentary:

1 Open Windows Live Photo Gallery and select the pictures required for the slide show

2 Click Make, Burn a DVD

3 The selected pictures are added to a new Windows DVD Maker project

4 Click Add Items for additional pictures

5 If desired, amend the DVD title (the default is the creation date) then click Next

6 Click Slide Show to change the settings for the show

199

7 Click Add Music to include sound in the slide show, select the tracks (or narrative audio) and click Add

8 Click Preview to check the slide show

Preview

9 Click Burn and insert a blank DVD to write the slide show to disc

Burn

Windows Live Movie Maker

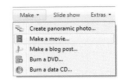

1 Choose the items that you require
from Windows Live Photo
Gallery, and then select the
command Make, Make a movie

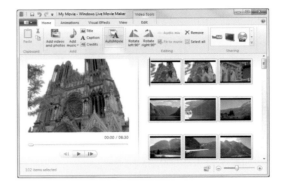

2 Click AutoMovie then follow the prompts to add
music and complete the movie

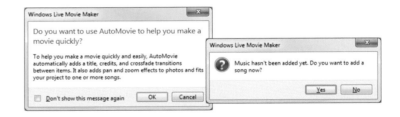

3 Make other changes to your movie as required

Windows Media Center

Windows Media Center offers integrated entertainment, with support for digital media of all types. With it you can listen to music or radio, watch TV, play a CD or DVD or manage your picture and video collections.

201

1 Click Start, All Programs and select Windows Media Center. The first time, Setup will run

2 The categories of media function are listed, including Pictures+Videos, Music, Movies, TV and Sports

3 Select Pictures+Videos to manage photos and video clips, sort by folder or tag etc, and play slide shows

...cont'd

4 Select Music for the Music library (and radio tuner)

5 Select Extras and then Explore to see more of the options available to you with media Player

6 There's also an Internet TV option that offers hit TV shows, movies, trailers and clips – all for free

13 Networking

Create a home network, wired or wireless, with a HomeGroup to share libraries and printers. Windows 7 computers can create or join a HomeGroup. You can also share network access with other systems such as Windows Vista or XP.

Create a Network

You have a network when you have several devices that exchange information over a wire or over radio waves. The simplest network consists of one computer and a router that links to the Internet. You can add a second computer, to share the Internet access and to exchange information with the other computer. If both computers are Windows 7 based, a HomeGroup can be established to make the sharing easier.

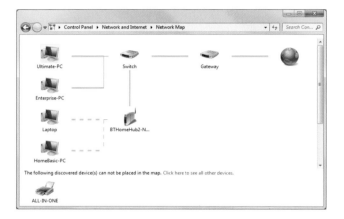

To make the connections your network will require:

1 Ethernet twisted-pair cables, for the wired portion

2 A router to manage the network connections

3 An Internet modem, which may be integrated with the router

4 An adapter for each computer (wired or wireless)

To implement your network, you'll need to carry out actions such as these:

- Install the necessary network adapters
- Establish the Internet Connection
- Set up the wireless router
- Connect the computers and start Windows

Network Location

1. Install the network adapter (if required) and start up Windows (with no network connection)

2. The icon on the system tray shows the adapter is currently disconnected

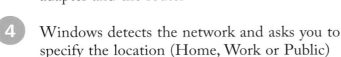

3. Add a cable between the adapter and the router

4. Windows detects the network and asks you to specify the location (Home, Work or Public)

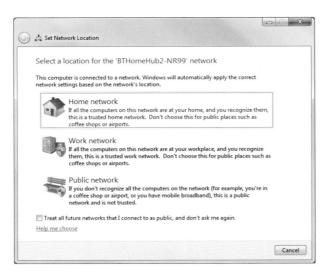

Choose **Home network** for your home network or in a known and trusted environment. The computer can belong to a HomeGroup, and Network discovery is turned on.

Choose **Work network** for small office or other workplace networks. Network discovery is turned on, so computers can see one another, but you can't create or join a HomeGroup.

Choose **Public network** for networks in places such as coffee shops or airports. HomeGroup is not available on public networks, and network discovery is turned off.

Don't forget

Often, there will be a network adapter built into your computer. Otherwise, you'll need to install an adapter card or add a USB network adapter.

Hot tip

Network discovery allows you to see other computers and devices on the network and allows other network users to see your computer. Turning Network discovery off hides your computer (see page 216).

Create HomeGroup

If you select Home, and no HomeGroup has yet been set up, you are given the option to create a HomeGroup

Don't forget

If a HomeGroup has already been created on the network, you get the option to join that HomeGroup (see page 211)

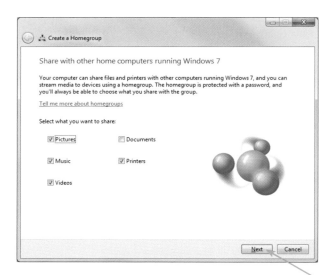

1 Specify what data you want to share then click Next

Hot tip

By default, you'll share your Pictures, Music, Videos and Printers, but not your Documents. However, you can add or remove any of these.

2 Record the password that Windows provides, to give to others joining the HomeGroup, and click Finish

Network and Sharing Center

1 Click the Network icon and select Open Network and Sharing Center

2 View Network setup details

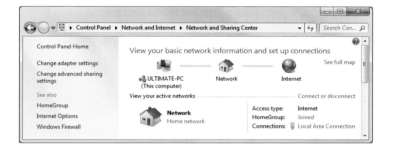

207

3 Scroll down to change your networking settings

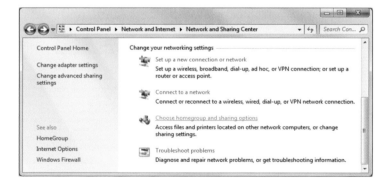

4 Click Choose HomeGroup and sharing options, to change HomeGroup settings or to view the password

Hot tip

Alternatively, select Start, Control Panel and click View network status and tasks, under Network and Internet.

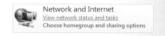

Hot tip

If you choose not to create the HomeGroup initially, you'll see the Ready to create option in the Network and Sharing Center.

Configure the Router

Use the wired connection on your computer to set up or reconfigure your router for Internet and wireless. The IP (Internet protocol) address should be recorded on the router label.

1 Open Internet Explorer and enter the address for your router, for example http://192.168.1.254

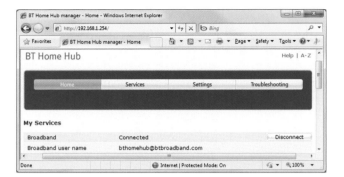

2 Type the administration password and click OK

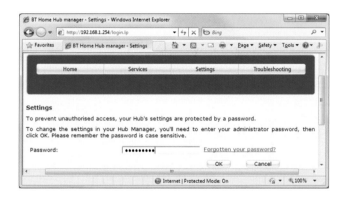

3 Select, for example, Settings and Wireless Setup

You can specify the wireless network name, the type of encryption and the encryption key, to improve the security of your network.

Wireless Connection

If your router includes wireless capability, you may decide to add a wireless adapter to your computer.

1 Insert the configuration CD for the wireless adapter and Run the setup program

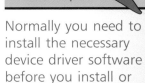
2 Click Here to Start, and then follow the prompts

3 The required files are installed on your computer

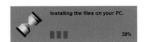

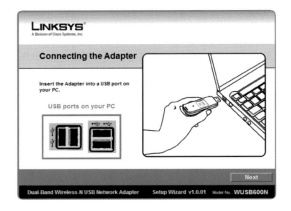

4 When prompted, insert your wireless adapter

Connect to Wireless Network

1 Click the network icon in the system tray

2 Choose your wireless network, select Connect automatically, and click Connect

3 Select Hide characters, then type the password for the network and click OK

4 Your computer will now show as connected to the wireless network

5 Right-click the entry for the wireless network and select Status

6 This will show the connection status, the speed, the signal quality and the amounts of data being transferred. Click Details to see the IP address assigned to the adapter

Join the HomeGroup

1 Connect the network cable (or select the wireless network and provide the required password)

2 Select the Home network location when prompted

3 Windows detects the existing HomeGroup and lets you select what you'd like to share with others

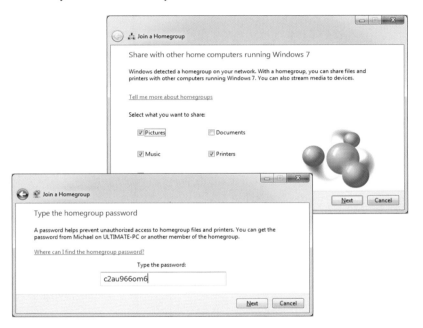

Don't forget

With Starter or Home Basic, Join is the only option you'll be offered, since Create HomeGroup isn't supported in these editions.

Hot tip

If you don't join immediately, the HomeGroup will be Available to join in the Network and Sharing Center.

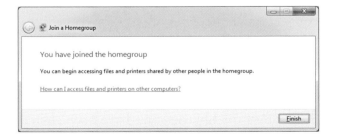

4 Type the HomeGroup password and click Next

5 You can now share data within the HomeGroup

Accessing the HomeGroup

To see a list of the computers that have joined as members of the HomeGroup on your network:

1 Select Start, click the User name and select the HomeGroup entry in the Navigation pane

2 Double-click one of the computers (or select the matching entry in the Navigation pane)

3 This shows the libraries that have been shared

4 Double-click a shared library to explore its contents, as you'd explore your own libraries

1 Create a new user account, log on as that user and select Start, type HomeGroup and press Enter

2 Select Start, User name and click the triangle next to HomeGroup to display the members

The new user has access to all of the shared libraries, including those belonging to the main user, but won't appear on the HomeGroup list unless that new user offers libraries to share.

To manage access to a specific file or folders

1 Select Start, click User name, navigate to the item, select it and click the Share With button

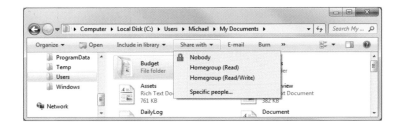

XP and Vista Computers

Don't forget

Computers using older versions of Windows cannot belong to the HomeGroup, but may still be found by Network discovery.

1 Select Start, click the user name and select the Network in the Navigation pane

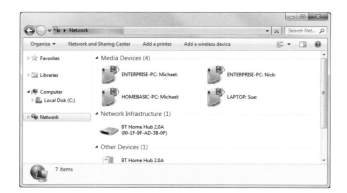

Hot tip

Initially, the Windows 7 HomeGroup appears and after a while Vista and XP computers are discovered.

2 Network computers are discovered and displayed

3 Expand the Network list and click on the Vista PC

Hot tip

Here the public folders and some printer devices are being shared.

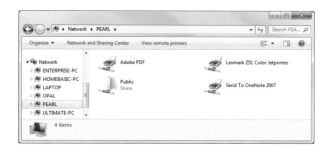

Network Map

1 Open the Network and Sharing Center and select the link to See full map

2 The message Windows is creating the network map is displayed for a few moments then the map appears

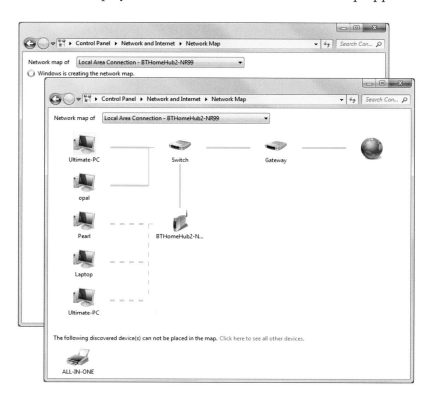

Windows may be unable to position some of the items that it discovers on the network, for example a wireless printer.

Don't forget

Click Start, type Network then select the Network and Sharing Center. You could also use the Network icon or the Control Panel (see page 90).

Hot tip

This shows computers running Windows 7 (Ultimate-PC and the Laptop), Windows XP (Opal) and Windows Vista (Pearl). PCs have either wired or wireless connections – or both, as shown for Ultimate-PC. The router appears as three components (switch, gateway and wireless access).

...cont'd

Hot tip

The network location you choose for your computer controls your visibility on the Network map and in the HomeGroup.

1 With the Home location, the computer will appear on the map and it may belong to the HomeGroup

2 With the Work location, the computer still appears on the map, but it cannot belong to the HomeGroup

3 For the Public location, the computer is not visible on the map and cannot belong to the HomeGroup

Don't forget

When you create the map from a computer that is Home or Work, it won't show Public computers that may be connected to the network.

4 Clicking Show full map gives the message Windows cannot create the map

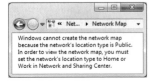

14 Security & Maintenance

Help and support is enhanced by online access to the latest information. There are also other ways of getting useful advice. Windows Action Center keeps track of your system, and a variety of system tools help protect your system from hazards.

Windows Help

Most functions in Windows are supported by wizards, which make the tasks easier by providing prompts and suggestions. However, there is a comprehensive help system when you do need answers to questions.

1 Click the Start button and select Help and Support

2 Select a topic, such as Learn about Windows Basics or view the Windows website

3 Click the Offline Help button and select Get online help, to be sure you get up-to-date help

4 Click Getting started with Windows 7 for some helpful videos on setting up your system

5 Scroll down and you'll see options to save or print the selected guide, plus a series of helpful articles

6 You can also search help information on your system

More Support Options

If you can't find the answer you are seeking in the Help information, ask someone else for help.

1 In Windows Help and Support, click the Ask button or click More support options

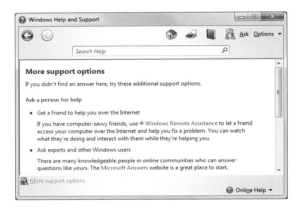

Don't forget

You can also use Windows Remote Assistance to offer your help to another user on the Internet.

2 Use Windows Remote Assistance to invite someone to access your system and help solve your problem

3 Post questions to the Windows communities, such as at the Microsoft Answers website

Hot tip

You are reminded about the Windows website (see page 218), and there is also a link to the more in-depth Microsoft TechNet website.

4 Search for your computer manufacturer's website, or contact Microsoft Customer Support online

Windows 7 Solution Center

Microsoft offers solution centers for many products, Windows 7 included. To visit this solution center:

1 Open http://support.microsoft.com, scroll down to the Solution Centers list and click Windows 7

Don't forget

The solution centers offered and the categories and topics listed will change from time to time, so revisit periodically.

2 Move the mouse pointer over a category, to see the list of topics covered, starting with Key resources

Hot tip

Right-click the topic and select Open in new tab or Open in new window, to keep the Solution Center available.

3 Display the Safety and security topics and select, for example, Windows Live Family Safety

Windows Action Center

There are a number of security and maintenance features in Windows 7, and these are monitored in the Windows Action Center. You'll be alerted by an icon in the notification area.

You can also open the Action Center by clicking Start, Control Panel, then Review your computer's status, under System and Security.

1 Click the icon to see the message summaries, then click Open Action Center

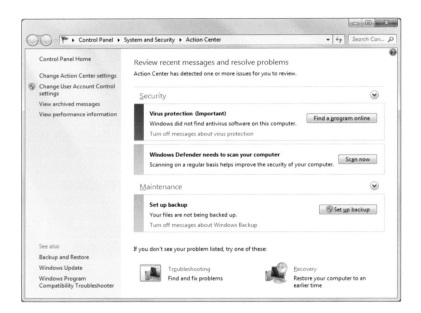

Red shows important items that should be dealt with quickly, such as antivirus software. Yellow items are suggested tasks such as maintenance activities.

2 Action Center warns you when there is no virus protection installed, marking this message Important

3 You may be reminded to run a scan using Windows Defender, antispyware software included in Windows

4 You will also be reminded if you have not set up any backup for your files

5 Action Center also has links to Troubleshooters and to System Restore (see page 230)

If there's no antivirus software installed:

1 Click the Find a program
button in the Action Center

2 Click a supplier on the list for details of Windows 7 compatible antivirus programs that are offered

There's usually a free trial version of the program. However, there are completely free versions, for example:

3 Visit free.grisoft.com to download AVG Free Edition, which is free for private, home use

4 When you've installed your chosen antivirus software, the warning message is removed from Action Center

Program Compatibility

Windows 7 helps you deal with older programs.

1 Right-click the Alerts icon and select Troubleshoot a problem, then select Run programs made for previous versions of Windows

Hot tip

You may also click Start, begin typing compatibility and select Run programs made for previous versions of Windows.

2 Click Next to search for problematic programs

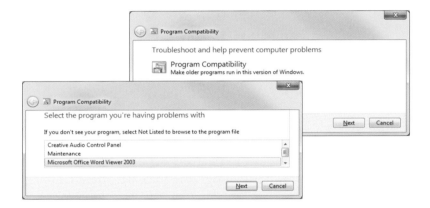

3 Find the program and try the recommended settings

Don't forget

The program may, for example, be run in Windows XP SP2 compatibility mode. If the results prove satisfactory, save the settings so that they will be used in future.

Windows XP Mode

If you have the Professional, Enterprise or Ultimate edition of Windows 7, there's another way to run older programs, using Windows Virtual PC and Windows XP Mode.

1 Go to www.microsoft.com/windows/virtual-pc/

Beware

Windows Virtual PC requires a CPU with the Intel Virtualization Technology or AMD-V feature. This feature must be enabled in the system BIOS.

2 Click the button to download these features

Hot tip

Download the release notes and the installation guide for more information on using Windows Virtual PC with Windows XP Mode and other operating systems.

3 Select system type (32-bit or 64-bit) and language, then follow the prompts to download and install Windows Virtual PC and Windows XP Mode

Windows Firewall

Hot tip

To protect your computer from malicious software while it is connected to the Internet, you need Firewall software. This is included as part of Windows.

1 Open Control Panel, System and Security and click Windows Firewall

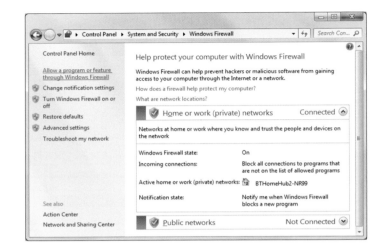

2 Click Allow a program or feature through Windows Firewall, to view the list of allowed programs

Don't forget

Programs may be added automatically when applications are installed, for example the AVG programs for providing daily updates.

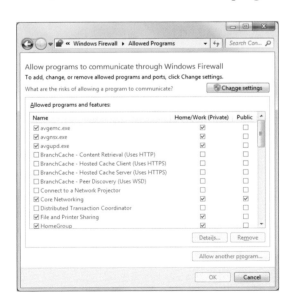

3 Click Change settings to add another program

Windows Defender

1 Select Start, type defender and click Windows Defender

2 Windows Defender opens and displays the latest status

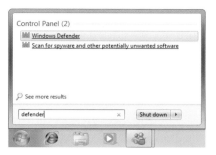

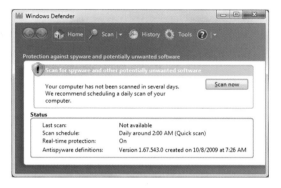

227

3 Click Scan now and Windows Defender will carry out a quick scan of your computer and report results

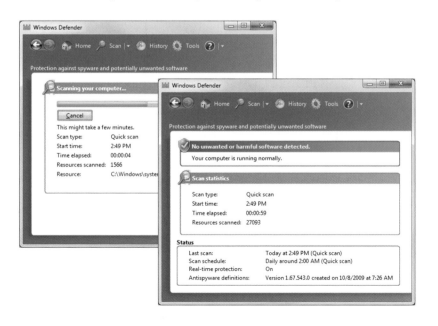

Windows Update

Hot tip

Updates are changes or additions that will help fix or prevent problems, enhance operation or improve performance.

To review the process by which software updates are added to Windows:

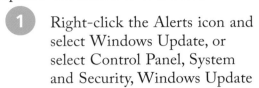

1 Right-click the Alerts icon and select Windows Update, or select Control Panel, System and Security, Windows Update

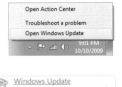

2 Windows displays the status, and gives a summary of the settings that are currently in effect

Beware

If Windows Update is not switched on, you'll see an alert in the Notification area.

3 Click here for details, to view the status of the Microsoft software notification for new programs

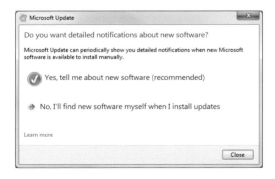

4 Amend the setting if desired, then click Close

...cont'd

1 Open Windows Update and select the Change Settings command

2 Windows Update shows the full list of settings, ready for any changes

Don't forget

Select Start, All Programs to open Windows Update from the Start menu.

Choose how Windows can install updates

When your computer is online, Windows can automatically check for important updates and install them using these settings. When new updates are available, you can also install them before shutting down the computer.

How does automatic updating help me?

Important updates

Install updates automatically (recommended)

Install new updates: Every day at 3:00 AM

Recommended updates

☑ Give me recommended updates the same way I receive important updates

Who can install updates

☑ Allow all users to install updates on this computer

Microsoft Update

☑ Give me updates for Microsoft products and check for new optional Microsoft software when I update Windows

Software notifications

☐ Show me detailed notifications when new Microsoft software is available

Note: Windows Update might update itself automatically first when checking for other updates. Read our privacy statement online.

OK   Cancel

229

3 Click the Important updates box and the list of options is displayed (with recommendations)

Install updates automatically (recommended)
Install updates automatically (recommended)
Download updates but let me choose whether to install them
Check for updates but let me choose whether to download and install them
Never check for updates (not recommended)

Hot tip

If you have a DSL connection, choose the Automatic option. Otherwise, select the Check for updates option.

4 Click the Install new updates box to select a particular day of the week

Every day
Every day
Every Sunday
Every Monday
Every Tuesday
Every Wednesday
Every Thursday
Every Friday
Every Saturday

5 You don't have to wait – if updates are ready you can open Windows Update and select Install Updates

Install updates

System Restore

Problems may arise when you install new software or a new device. If uninstalling does not correct the situation, you can return the system files to their values prior to the changes.

Restore points are created every day and just before any significant change such as an installation or update. You can also open System Protection and create a restore point yourself.

1 Click Start, type system restore and press Enter

2 System Restore will offer to reverse the most recent change (the best choice)

3 To see what other restore points are available, click Choose a different restore point and click Next

Select a date and time that's prior to the problems and click Next to apply the change.

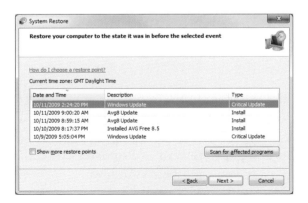

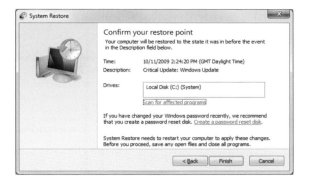

Don't forget

Once started, System Restore cannot be interrupted, though it can be undone (unless run from Safe Mode or the System Recovery menu).

4 Click Finish to confirm your selected restore point

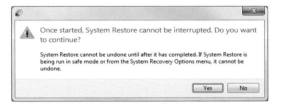

231

5 On restart, System Restore confirms restore

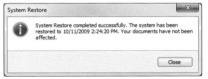

6 You can still run System Restore to undo the restore

Hot tip

If the selected restore point does not resolve your problems, you can undo the restore, or try a different restore point.

Backup and Restore

You can lose files accidentally, as a result of a virus, or due to software or hardware failure. To protect your files, you should make backup copies.

1 Click Start, All Programs, Maintenance, Backup and Restore Center

2 The first time, you'll need to select Set up backup

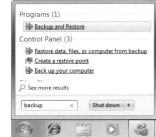

3 Choose an external drive if possible, on the computer or on another computer on the network

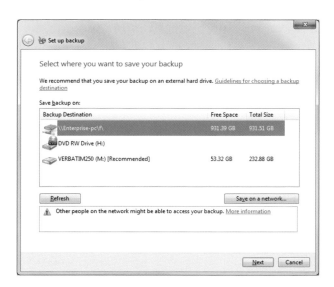

Index

Index

G

H

I

X

Z

U

V

W

X

Z